# CHAPTER O



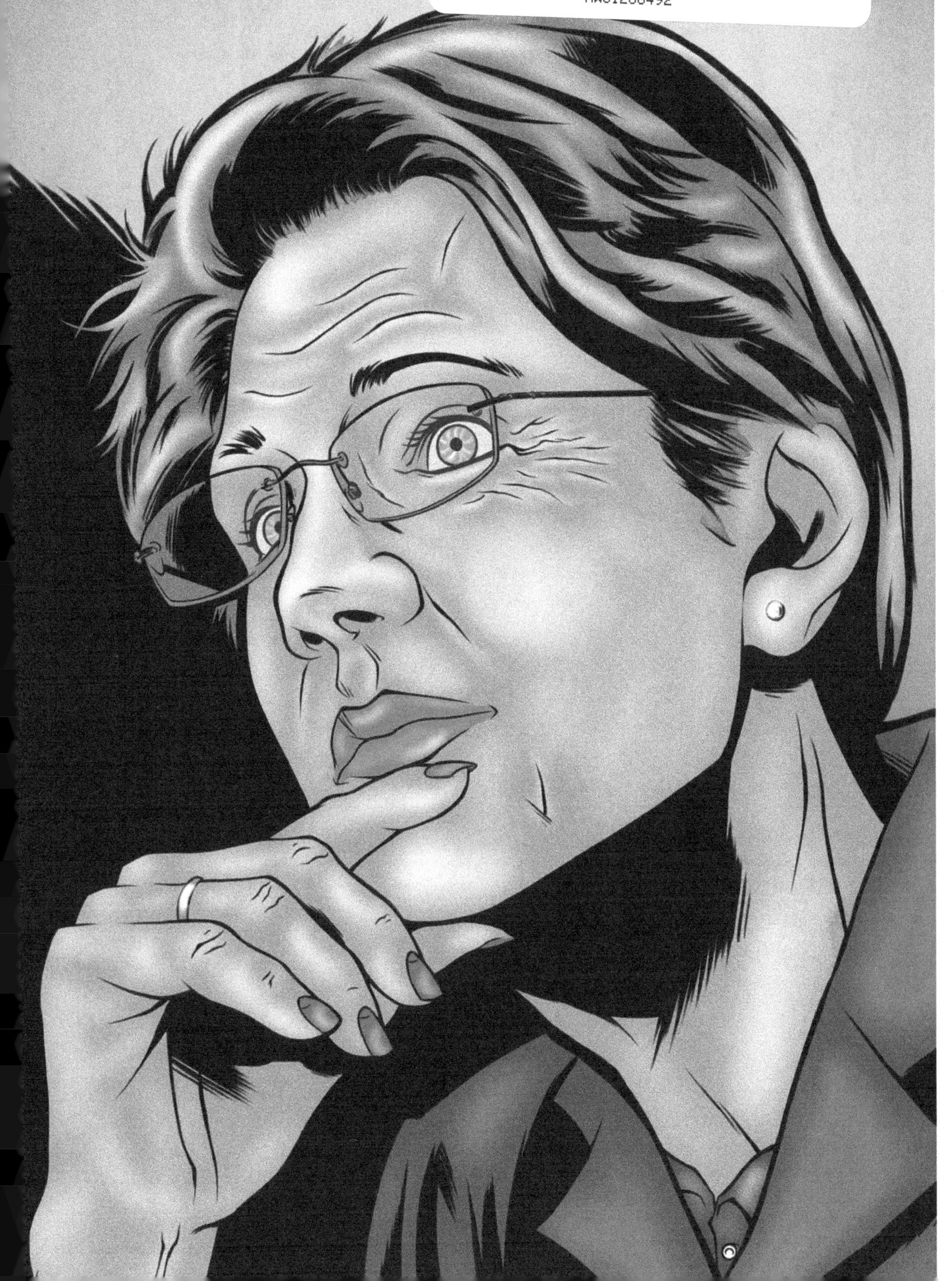

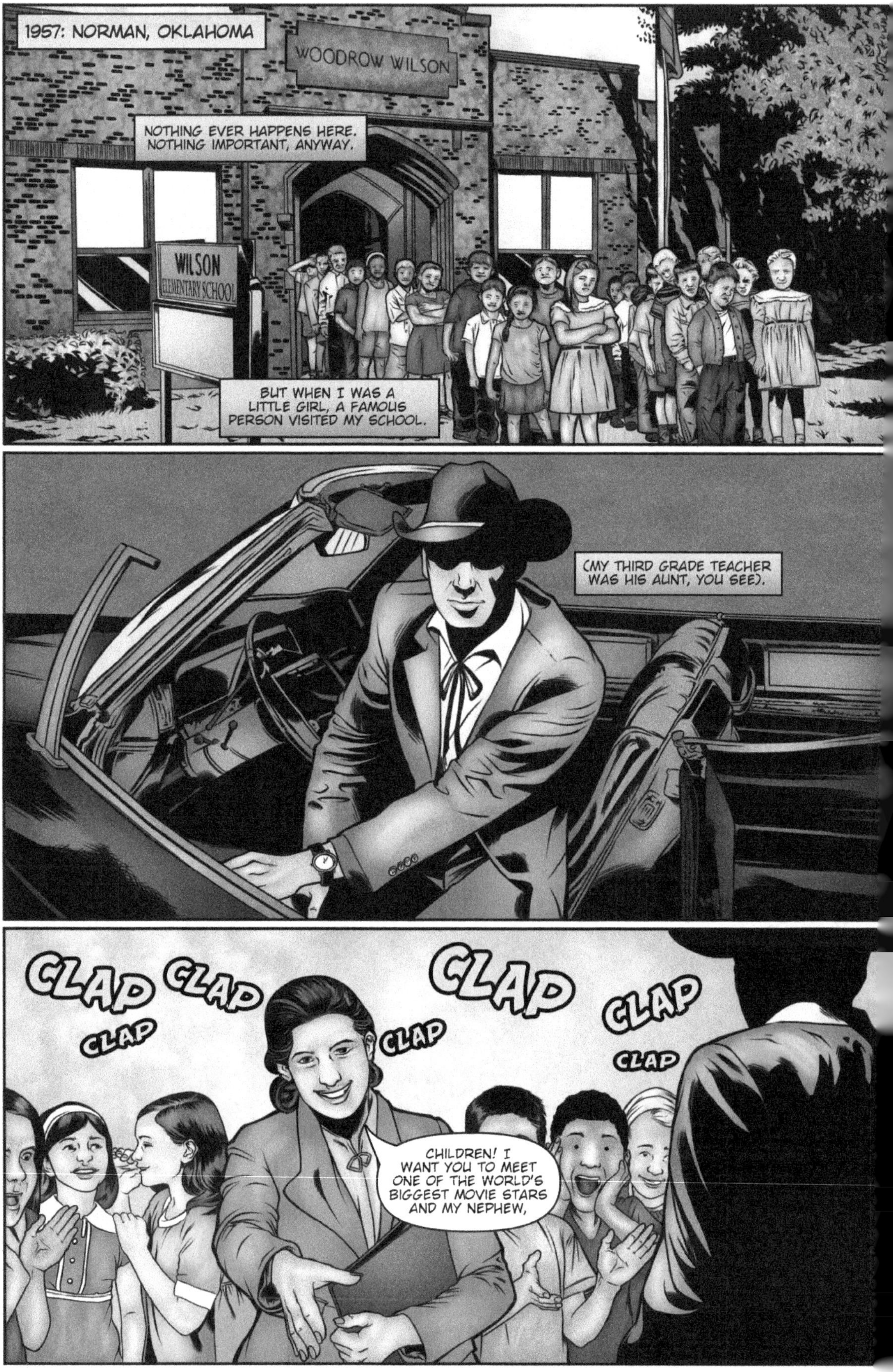
1957: NORMAN, OKLAHOMA
WOODROW WILSON
NOTHING EVER HAPPENS HERE. NOTHING IMPORTANT, ANYWAY.
WILSON ELEMENTARY SCHOOL
BUT WHEN I WAS A LITTLE GIRL, A FAMOUS PERSON VISITED MY SCHOOL.
(MY THIRD GRADE TEACHER WAS HIS AUNT, YOU SEE).
CLAP CLAP CLAP CLAP CLAP CLAP CLAP
CHILDREN! I WANT YOU TO MEET ONE OF THE WORLD'S BIGGEST MOVIE STARS AND MY NEPHEW,

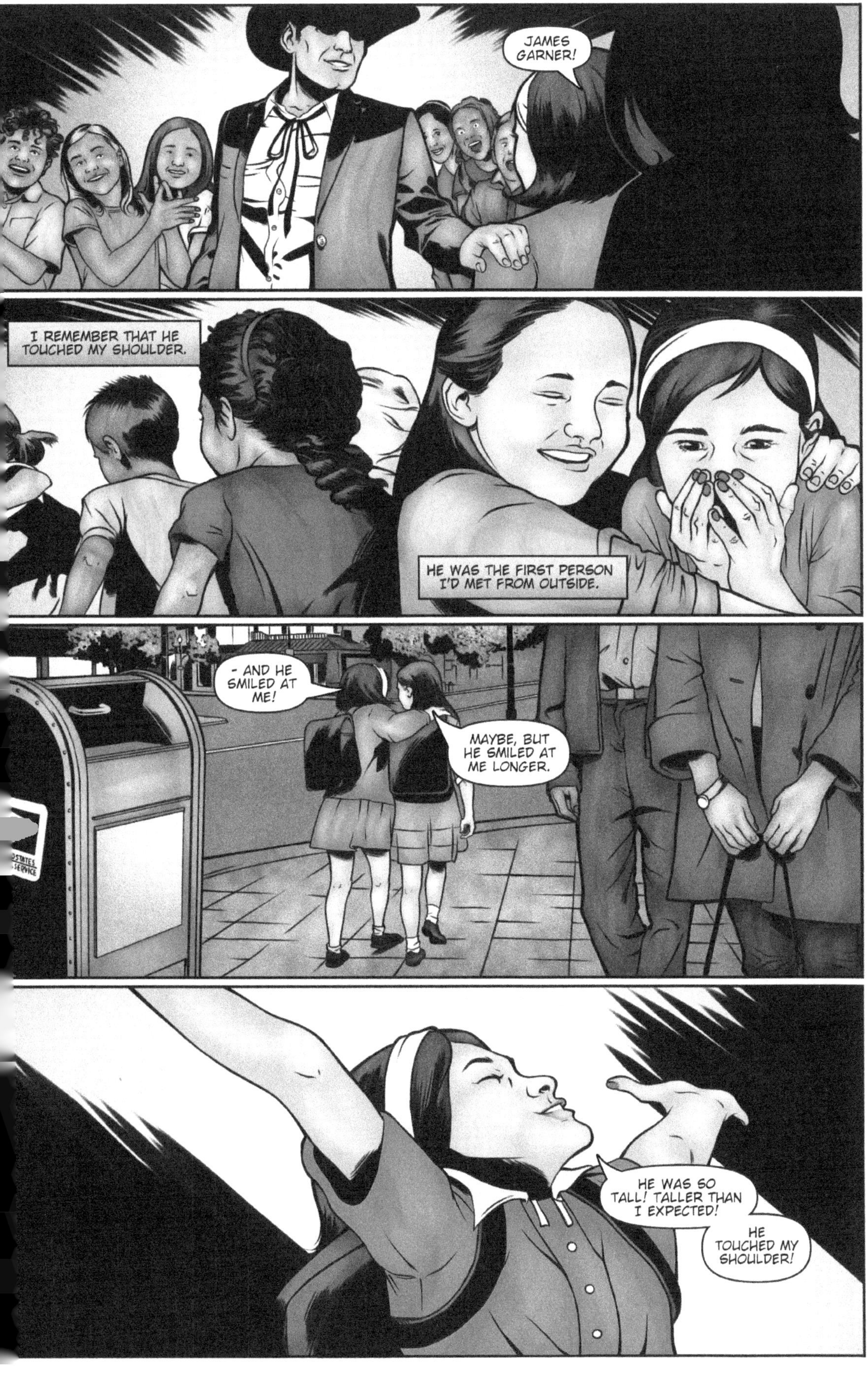
JAMES GARNER!
I REMEMBER THAT HE TOUCHED MY SHOULDER.
HE WAS THE FIRST PERSON I'D MET FROM OUTSIDE.
- AND HE SMILED AT ME!
MAYBE, BUT HE SMILED AT ME LONGER.
HE WAS SO TALL! TALLER THAN I EXPECTED!
HE TOUCHED MY SHOULDER!

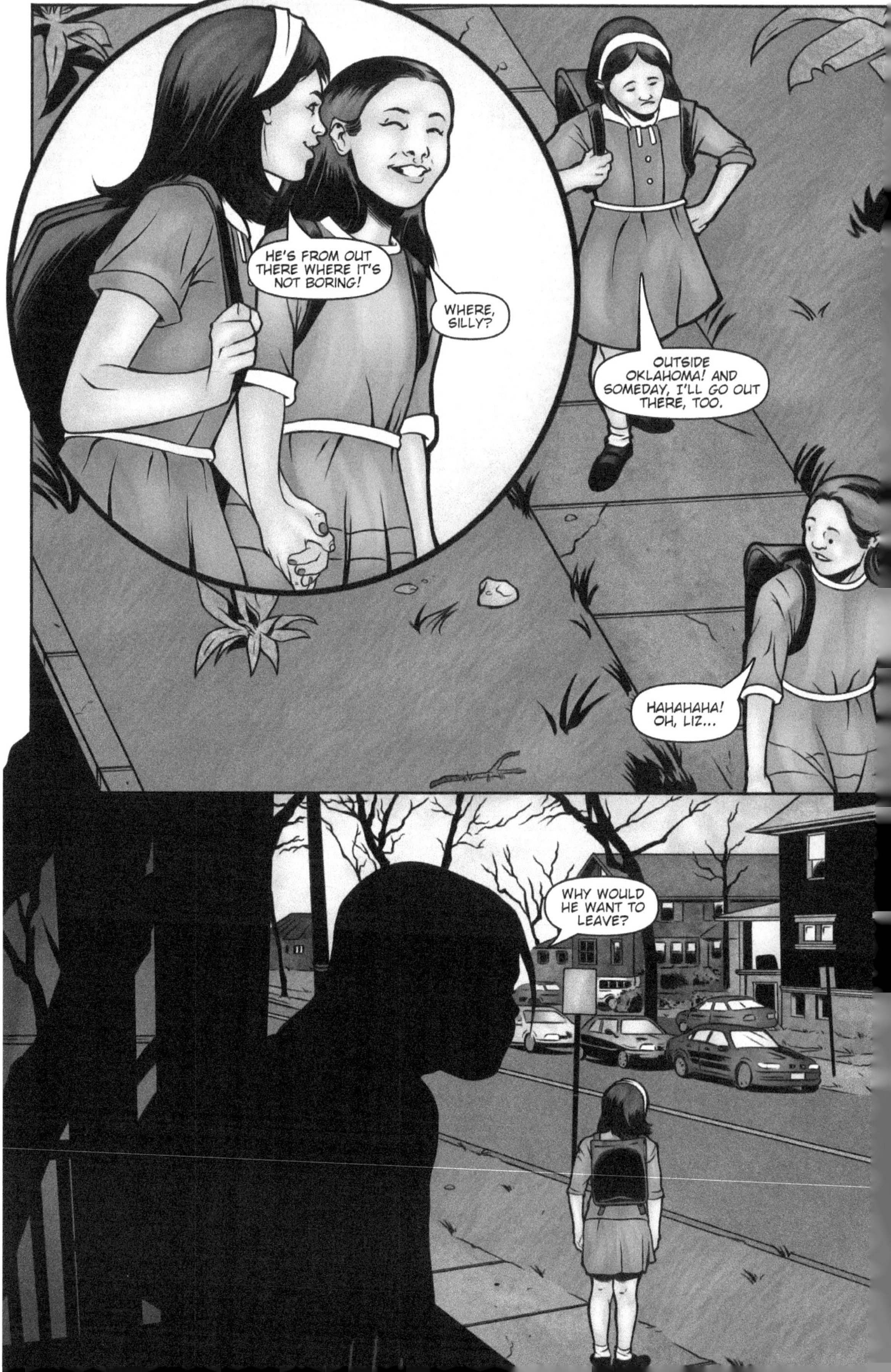
HE'S FROM OUT THERE WHERE IT'S NOT BORING!
WHERE, SILLY?
OUTSIDE OKLAHOMA! AND SOMEDAY, I'LL GO OUT THERE, TOO.
HAHAHAHA! OH, LIZ...
WHY WOULD HE WANT TO LEAVE?

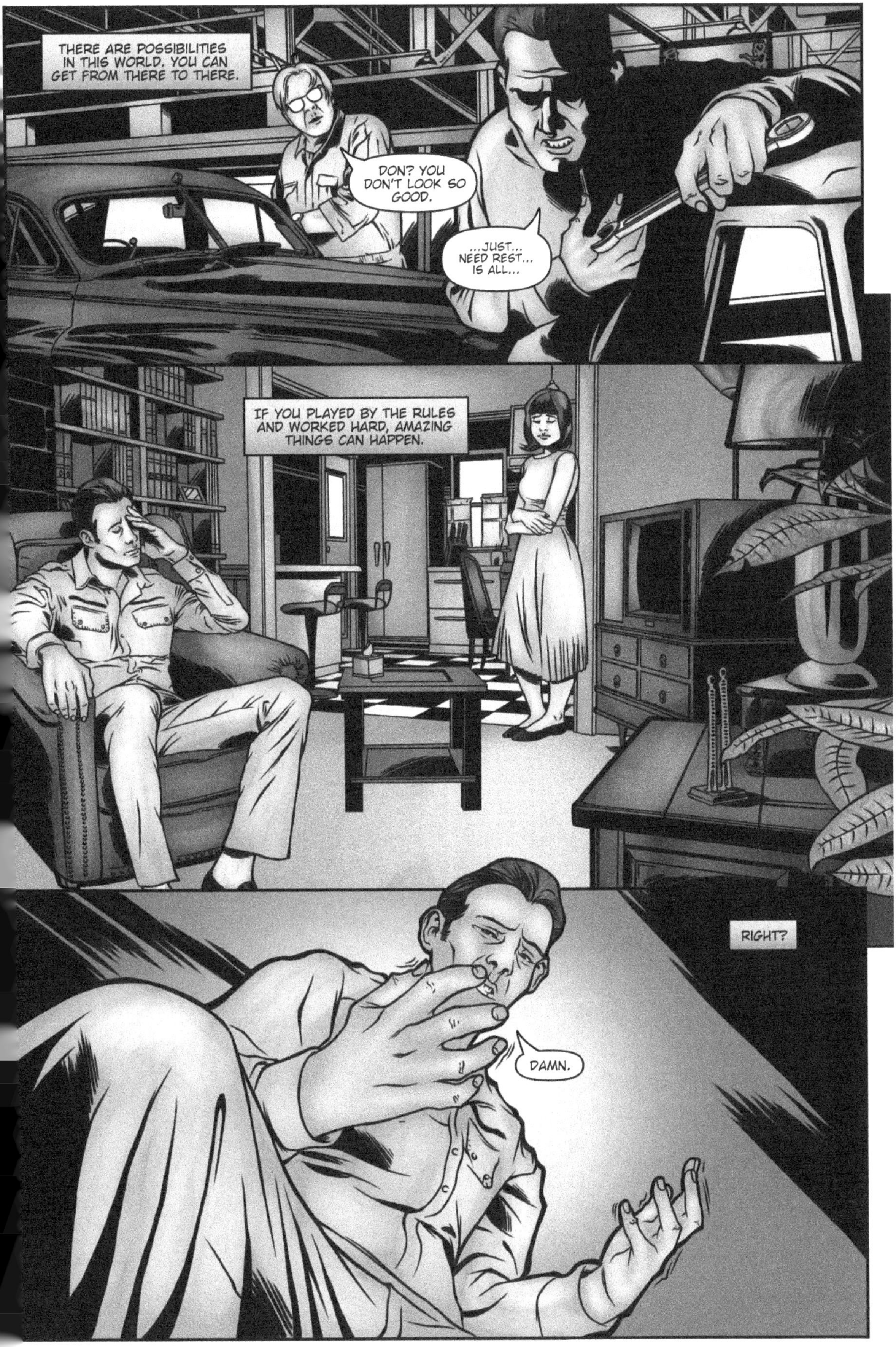
THERE ARE POSSIBILITIES IN THIS WORLD. YOU CAN GET FROM THERE TO THERE.
DON? YOU DON'T LOOK SO GOOD.
...JUST... NEED REST... IS ALL...
IF YOU PLAYED BY THE RULES AND WORKED HARD, AMAZING THINGS CAN HAPPEN.
RIGHT?
DAMN.

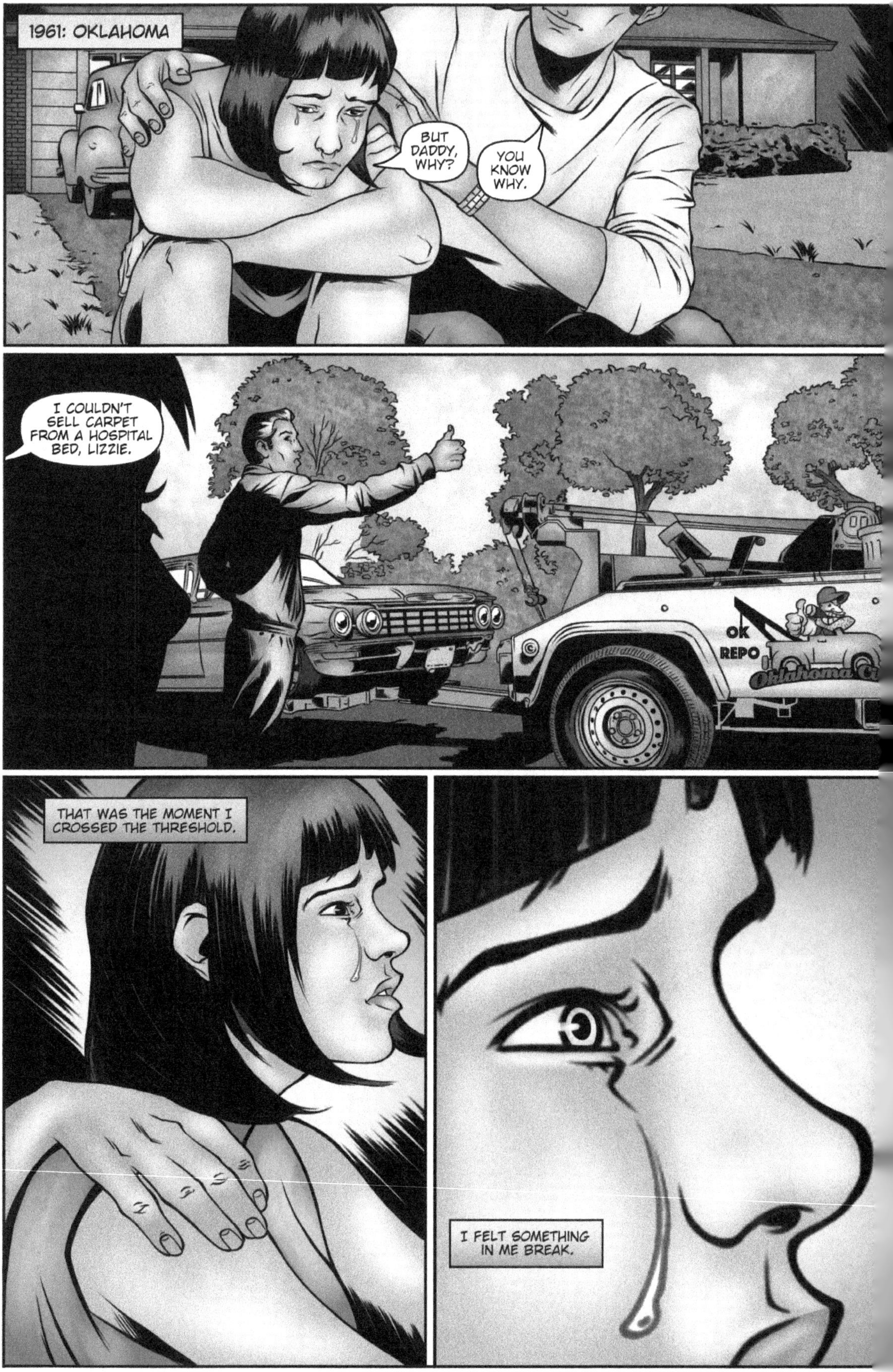
1961: OKLAHOMA
BUT DADDY, WHY?
YOU KNOW WHY.
I COULDN'T SELL CARPET FROM A HOSPITAL BED, LIZZIE.
OK REPO
THAT WAS THE MOMENT I CROSSED THE THRESHOLD.
I FELT SOMETHING IN ME BREAK.

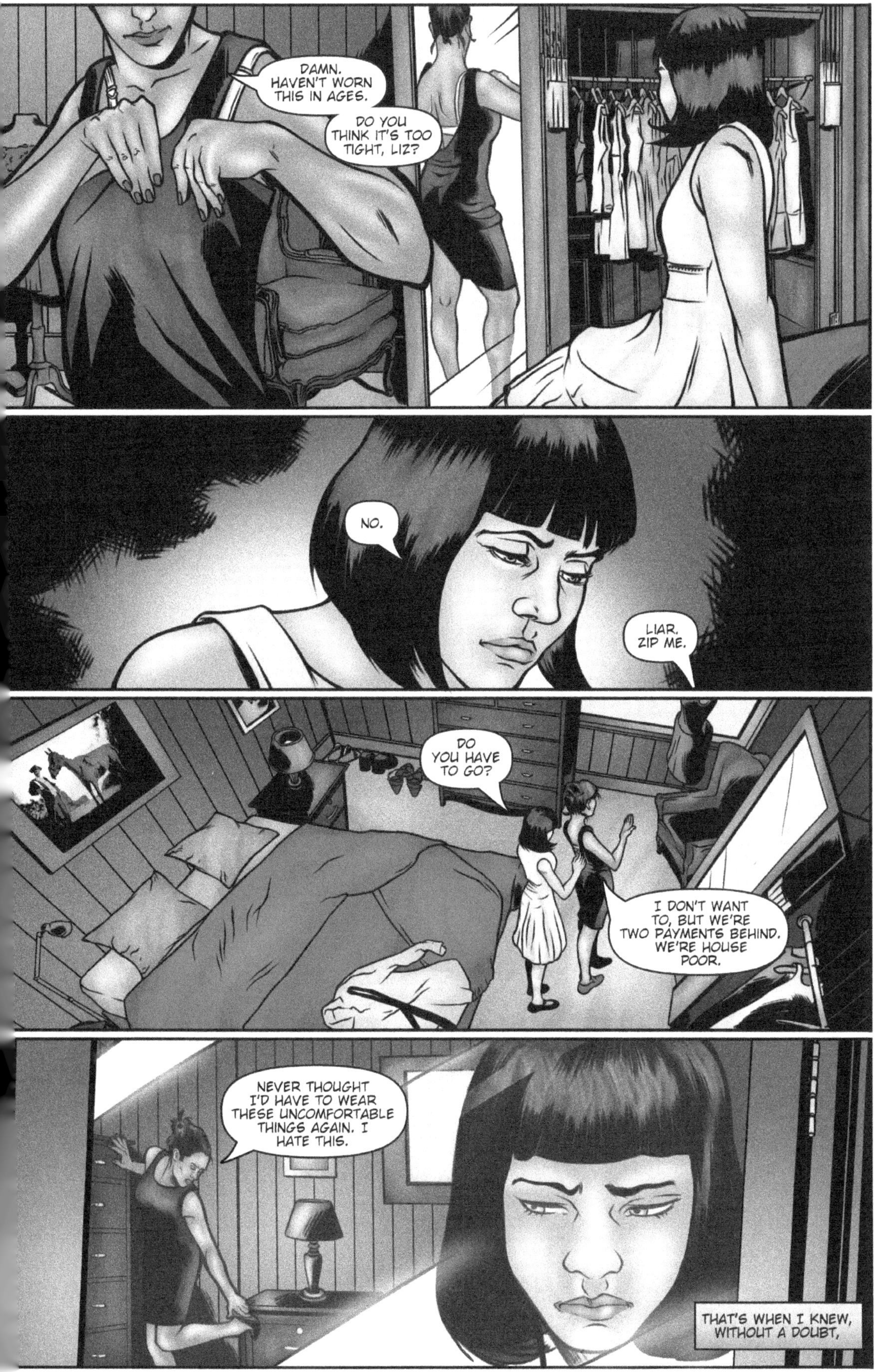

DAMN. HAVEN'T WORN THIS IN AGES.
DO YOU THINK IT'S TOO TIGHT, LIZ?
NO.
LIAR. ZIP ME.
DO YOU HAVE TO GO?
I DON'T WANT TO, BUT WE'RE TWO PAYMENTS BEHIND. WE'RE HOUSE POOR.
NEVER THOUGHT I'D HAVE TO WEAR THESE UNCOMFORTABLE THINGS AGAIN. I HATE THIS.
THAT'S WHEN I KNEW, WITHOUT A DOUBT,

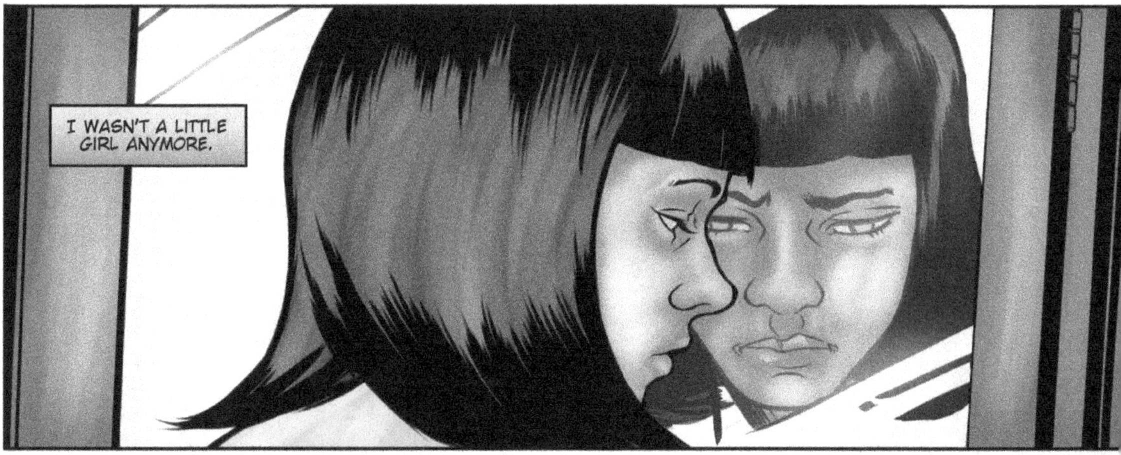
I WASN'T A LITTLE GIRL ANYMORE.

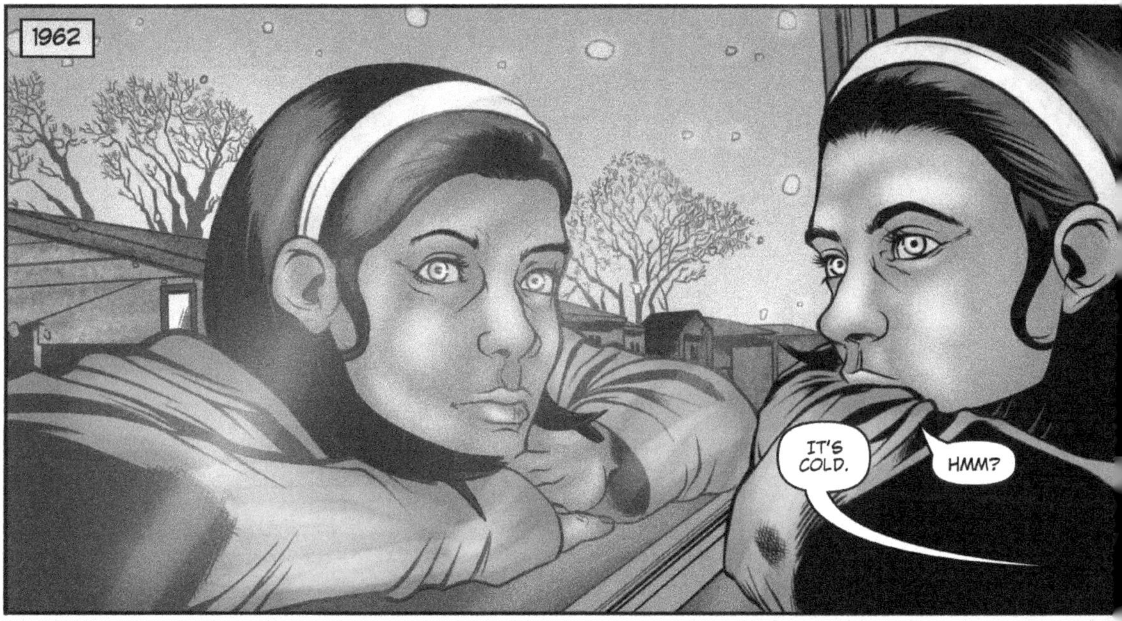
1962
IT'S COLD.
HMM?

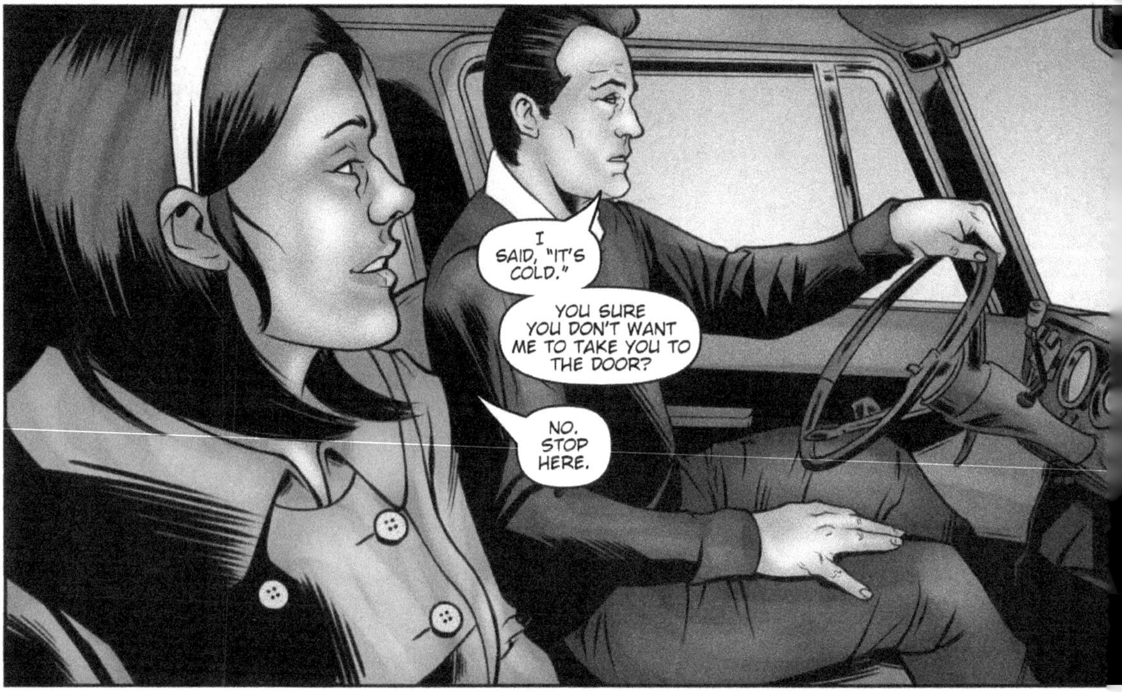
I SAID, "IT'S COLD."
YOU SURE YOU DON'T WANT ME TO TAKE YOU TO THE DOOR?
NO. STOP HERE.

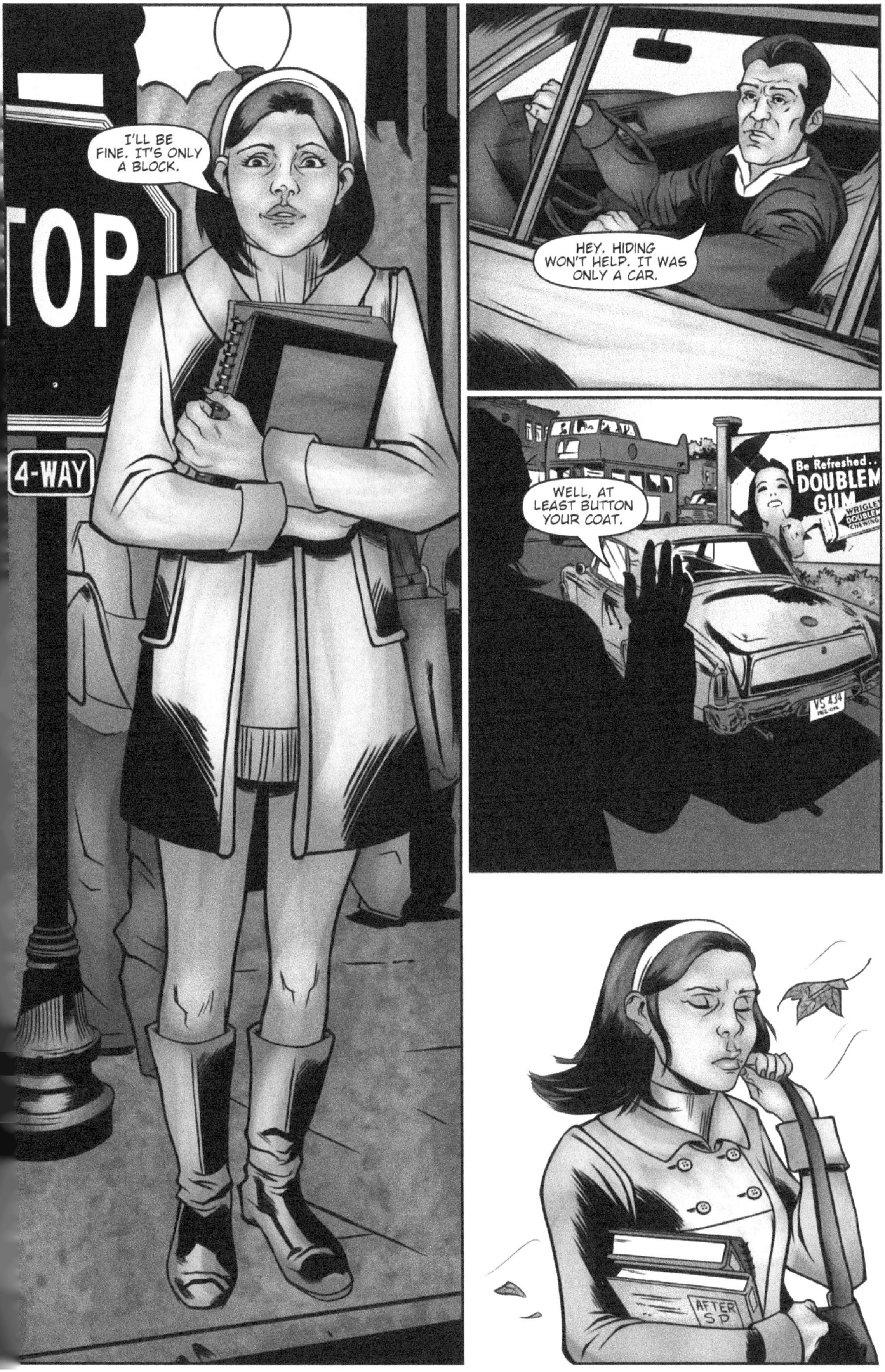
I'LL BE FINE. IT'S ONLY A BLOCK.
4-WAY
HEY. HIDING WON'T HELP. IT WAS ONLY A CAR.
Be Refreshed..
WELL, AT LEAST BUTTON YOUR COAT.

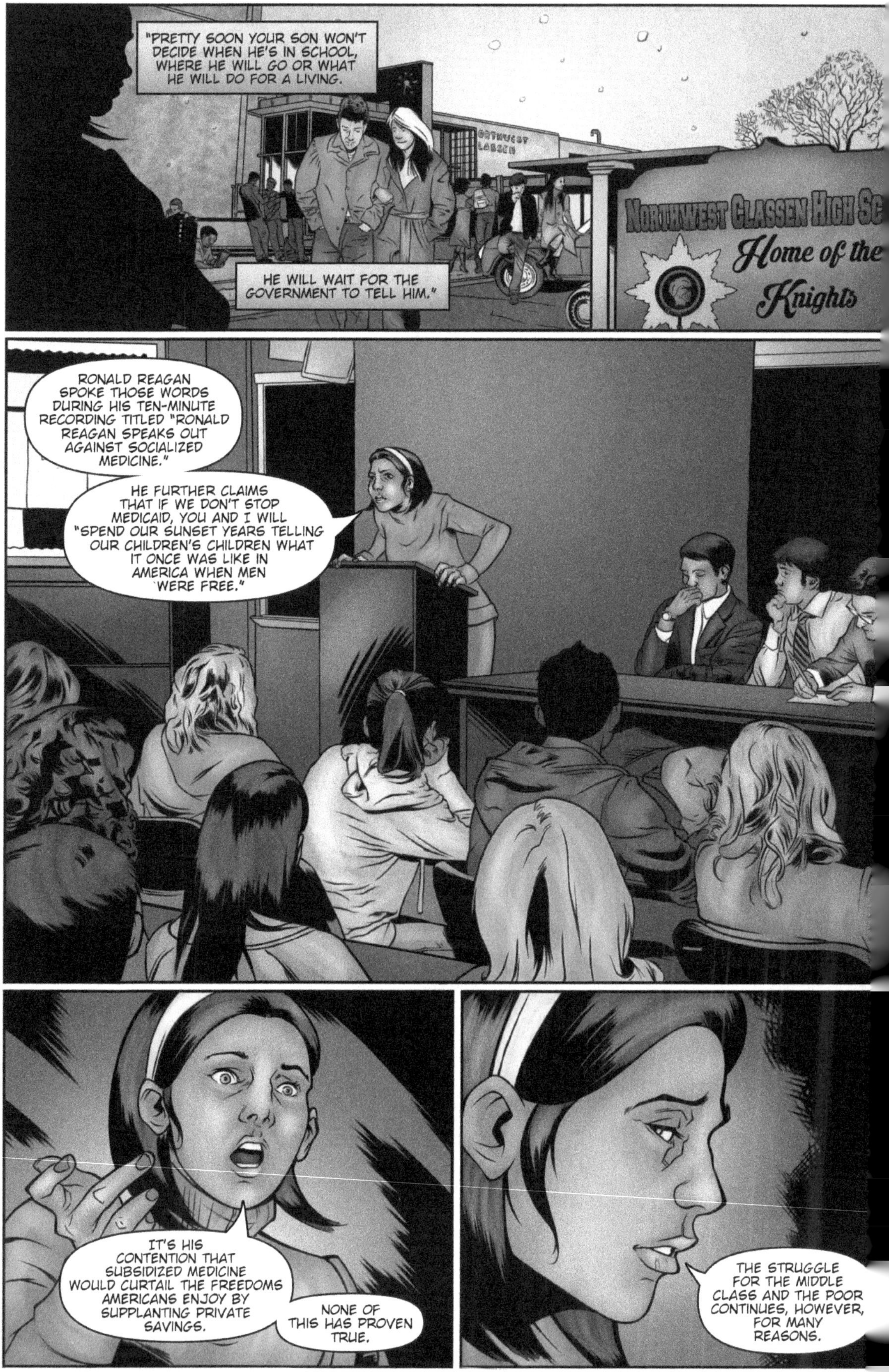
"PRETTY SOON YOUR SON WON'T DECIDE WHEN HE'S IN SCHOOL, WHERE HE WILL GO OR WHAT HE WILL DO FOR A LIVING.
NORTHWEST CLASSEN HIGH SC
Home of the Knights
HE WILL WAIT FOR THE GOVERNMENT TO TELL HIM."
RONALD REAGAN SPOKE THOSE WORDS DURING HIS TEN-MINUTE RECORDING TITLED "RONALD REAGAN SPEAKS OUT AGAINST SOCIALIZED MEDICINE."
HE FURTHER CLAIMS THAT IF WE DON'T STOP MEDICAID, YOU AND I WILL "SPEND OUR SUNSET YEARS TELLING OUR CHILDREN'S CHILDREN WHAT IT ONCE WAS LIKE IN AMERICA WHEN MEN WERE FREE."
IT'S HIS CONTENTION THAT SUBSIDIZED MEDICINE WOULD CURTAIL THE FREEDOMS AMERICANS ENJOY BY SUPPLANTING PRIVATE SAVINGS.
NONE OF THIS HAS PROVEN TRUE.
THE STRUGGLE FOR THE MIDDLE CLASS AND THE POOR CONTINUES, HOWEVER, FOR MANY REASONS.

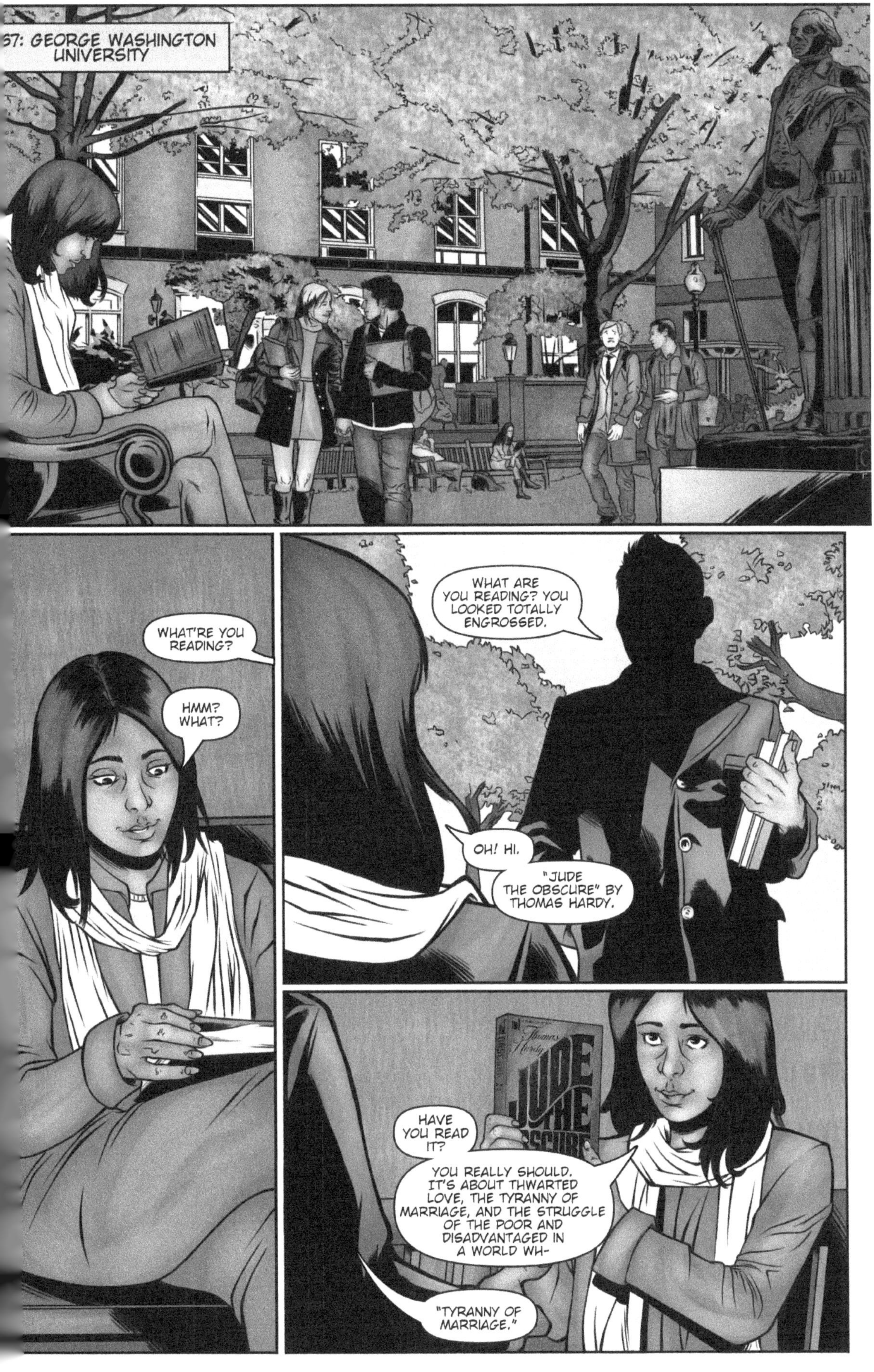

67: GEORGE WASHINGTON UNIVERSITY
WHAT'RE YOU READING?
HMM? WHAT?
WHAT ARE YOU READING? YOU LOOKED TOTALLY ENGROSSED.
OH! HI.
"JUDE THE OBSCURE" BY THOMAS HARDY.
Thomas Hardy
JUDE THE OBSCURE
HAVE YOU READ IT?
YOU REALLY SHOULD. IT'S ABOUT THWARTED LOVE, THE TYRANNY OF MARRIAGE, AND THE STRUGGLE OF THE POOR AND DISADVANTAGED IN A WORLD WH-
"TYRANNY OF MARRIAGE."

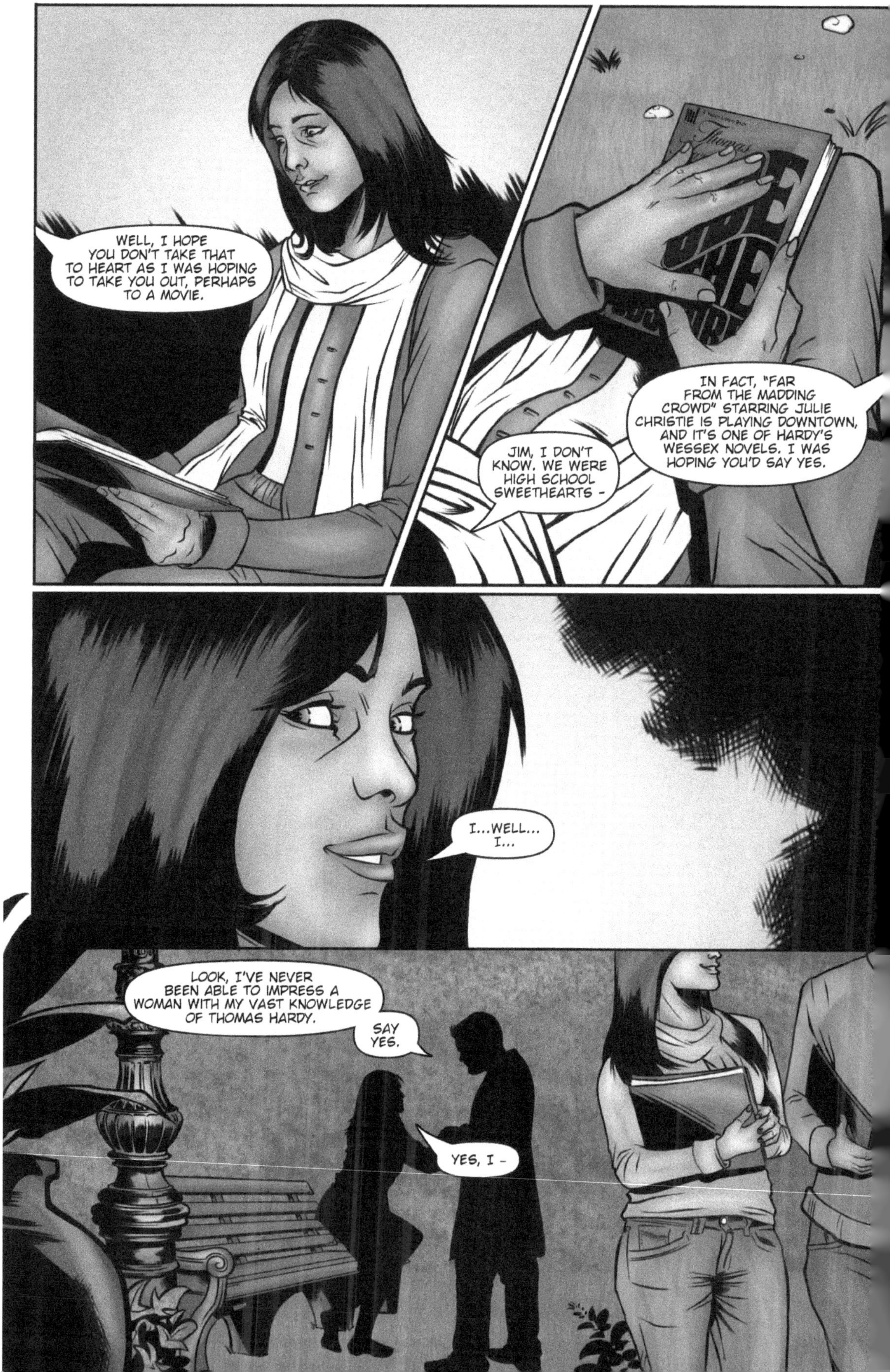
WELL, I HOPE YOU DON'T TAKE THAT TO HEART AS I WAS HOPING TO TAKE YOU OUT, PERHAPS TO A MOVIE.
IN FACT, "FAR FROM THE MADDING CROWD" STARRING JULIE CHRISTIE IS PLAYING DOWNTOWN, AND IT'S ONE OF HARDY'S WESSEX NOVELS. I WAS HOPING YOU'D SAY YES.
JIM, I DON'T KNOW. WE WERE HIGH SCHOOL SWEETHEARTS -
I...WELL... I...
LOOK, I'VE NEVER BEEN ABLE TO IMPRESS A WOMAN WITH MY VAST KNOWLEDGE OF THOMAS HARDY.
SAY YES.
YES, I -

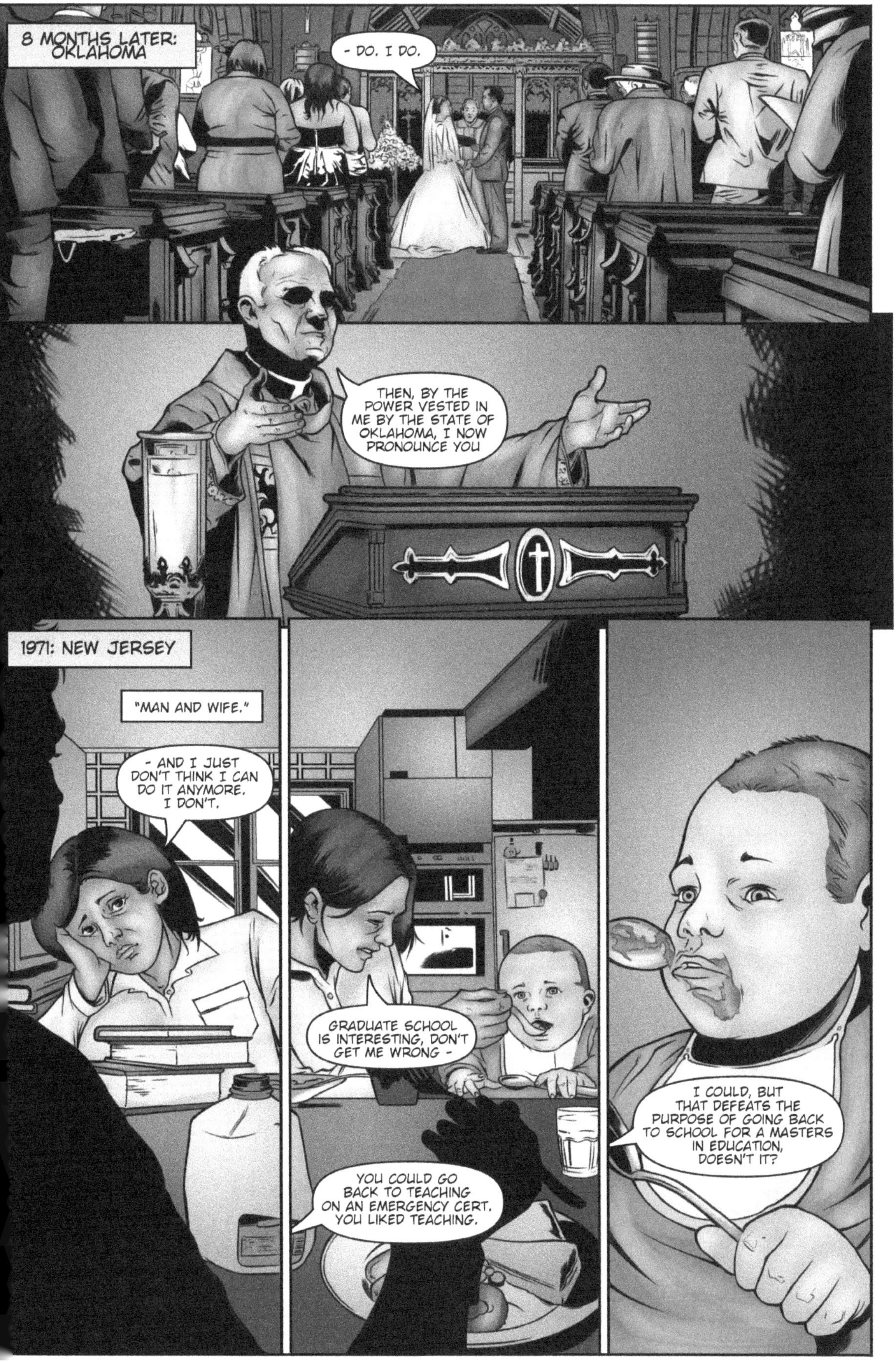
8 MONTHS LATER: OKLAHOMA
- DO. I DO.
THEN, BY THE POWER VESTED IN ME BY THE STATE OF OKLAHOMA, I NOW PRONOUNCE YOU
1971: NEW JERSEY
"MAN AND WIFE."
- AND I JUST DON'T THINK I CAN DO IT ANYMORE. I DON'T.
GRADUATE SCHOOL IS INTERESTING, DON'T GET ME WRONG -
YOU COULD GO BACK TO TEACHING ON AN EMERGENCY CERT. YOU LIKED TEACHING.
I COULD, BUT THAT DEFEATS THE PURPOSE OF GOING BACK TO SCHOOL FOR A MASTERS IN EDUCATION, DOESN'T IT?

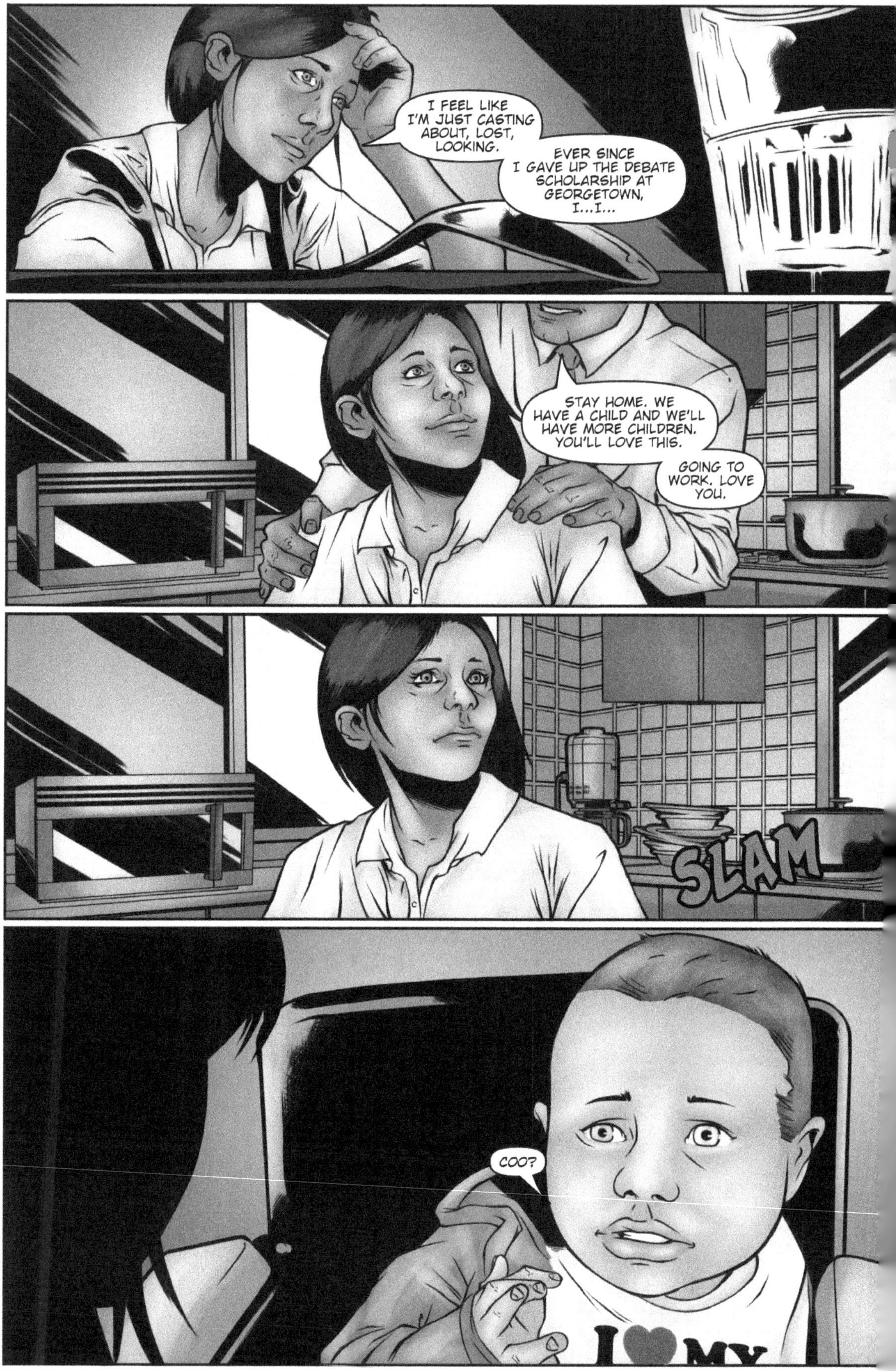
I FEEL LIKE I'M JUST CASTING ABOUT, LOST, LOOKING.
EVER SINCE I GAVE UP THE DEBATE SCHOLARSHIP AT GEORGETOWN, I...I...
STAY HOME. WE HAVE A CHILD AND WE'LL HAVE MORE CHILDREN. YOU'LL LOVE THIS.
GOING TO WORK. LOVE YOU.
SLAM
COO?
I MY

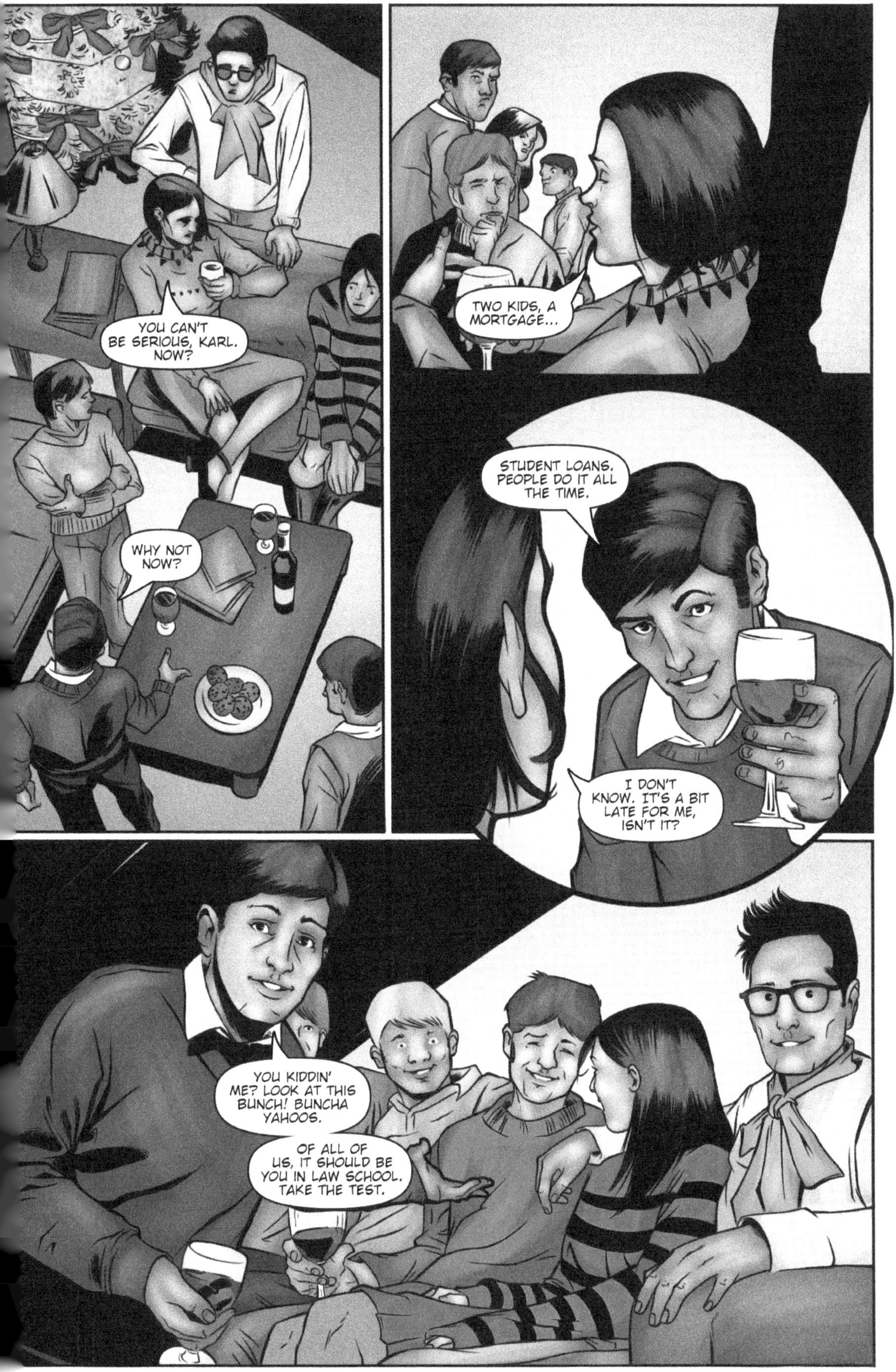
YOU CAN'T BE SERIOUS, KARL. NOW?
WHY NOT NOW?
TWO KIDS, A MORTGAGE...
STUDENT LOANS. PEOPLE DO IT ALL THE TIME.
I DON'T KNOW. IT'S A BIT LATE FOR ME, ISN'T IT?
YOU KIDDIN' ME? LOOK AT THIS BUNCH! BUNCHA YAHOOS.
OF ALL OF US, IT SHOULD BE YOU IN LAW SCHOOL. TAKE THE TEST.

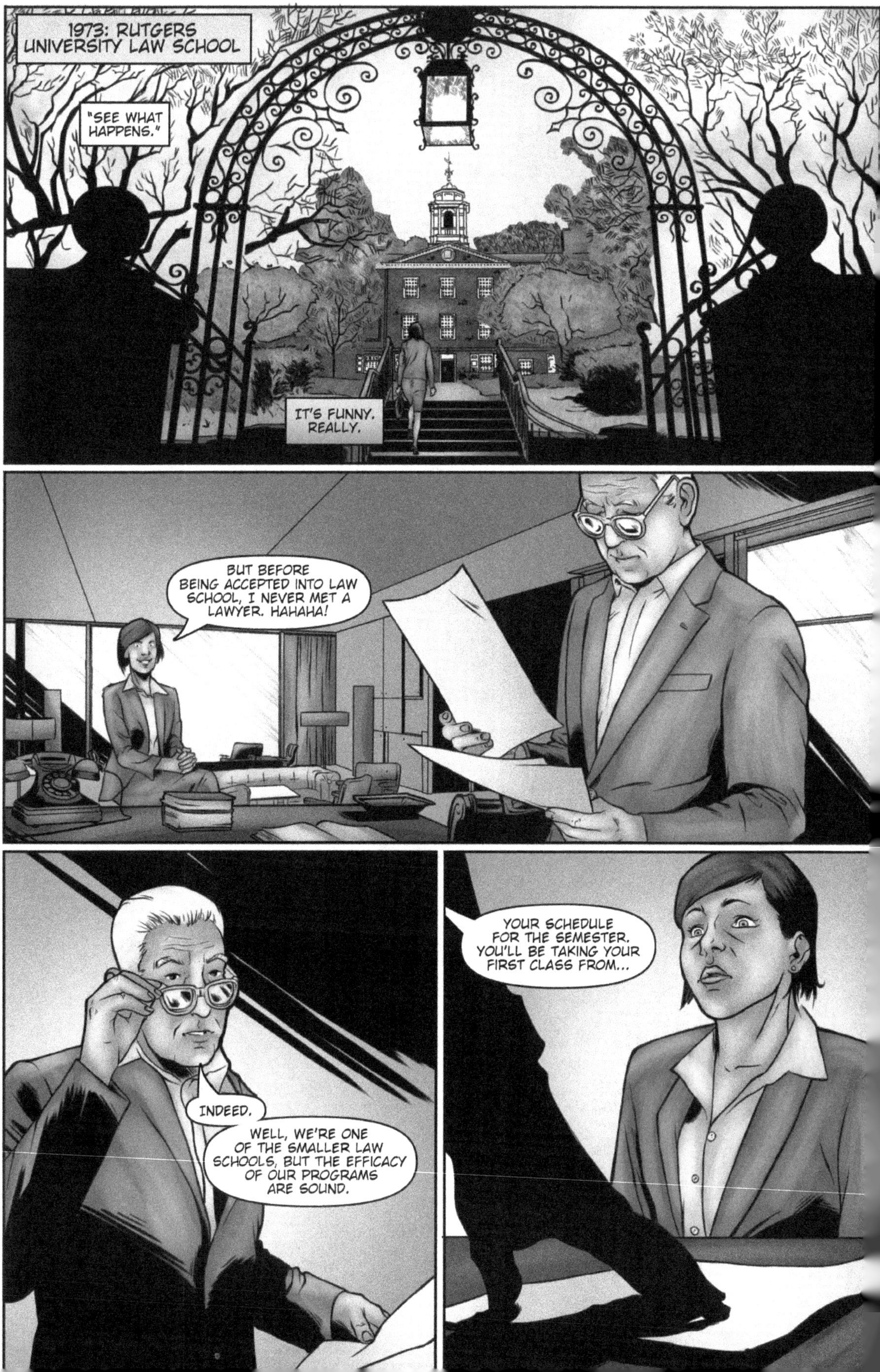
1973: RUTGERS UNIVERSITY LAW SCHOOL
"SEE WHAT HAPPENS."
IT'S FUNNY. REALLY.
BUT BEFORE BEING ACCEPTED INTO LAW SCHOOL, I NEVER MET A LAWYER. HAHAHA!
INDEED.
WELL, WE'RE ONE OF THE SMALLER LAW SCHOOLS, BUT THE EFFICACY OF OUR PROGRAMS ARE SOUND.
YOUR SCHEDULE FOR THE SEMESTER. YOU'LL BE TAKING YOUR FIRST CLASS FROM...

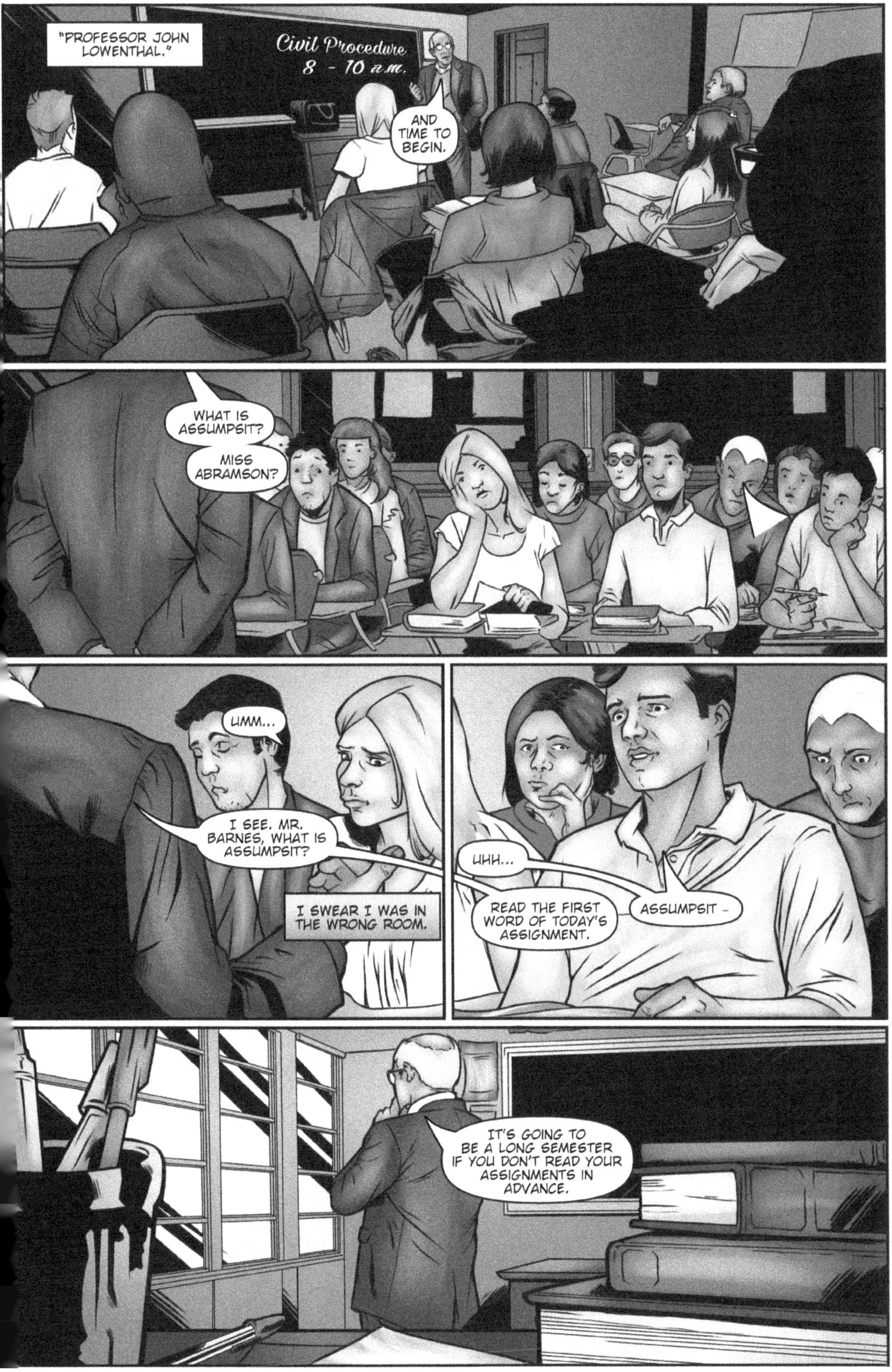
"PROFESSOR JOHN LOWENTHAL."
Civil Procedure 8 - 10 a.m.
AND TIME TO BEGIN.
WHAT IS ASSUMPSIT?
MISS ABRAMSON?
UMM...
I SEE. MR. BARNES, WHAT IS ASSUMPSIT?
I SWEAR I WAS IN THE WRONG ROOM.
UHH...
ASSUMPSIT –
READ THE FIRST WORD OF TODAY'S ASSIGNMENT.
IT'S GOING TO BE A LONG SEMESTER IF YOU DON'T READ YOUR ASSIGNMENTS IN ADVANCE.

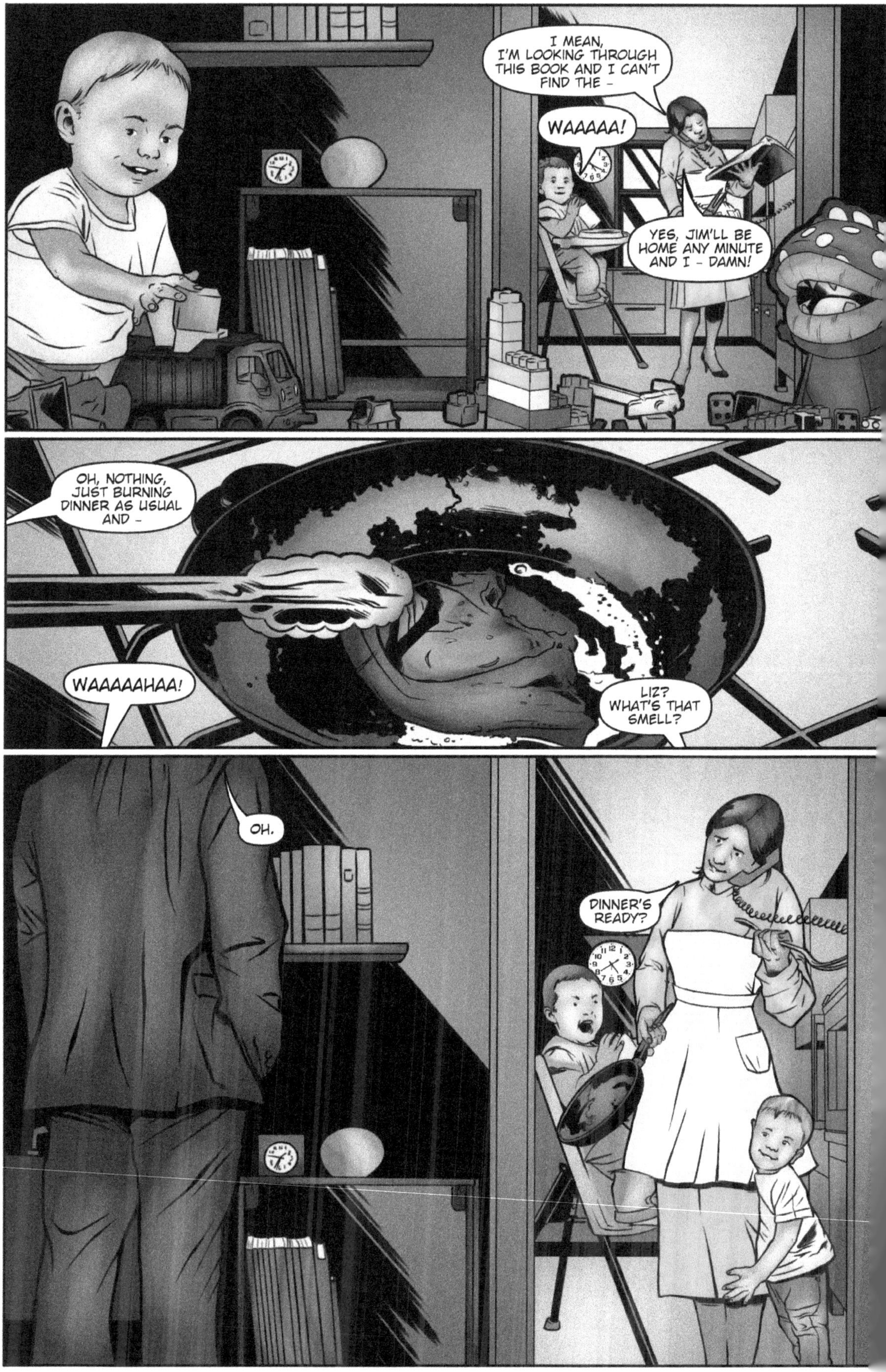
I MEAN, I'M LOOKING THROUGH THIS BOOK AND I CAN'T FIND THE -
WAAAAA!
YES, JIM'LL BE HOME ANY MINUTE AND I - DAMN!
OH, NOTHING, JUST BURNING DINNER AS USUAL AND -
WAAAAAHAA!
LIZ? WHAT'S THAT SMELL?
OH.
DINNER'S READY?

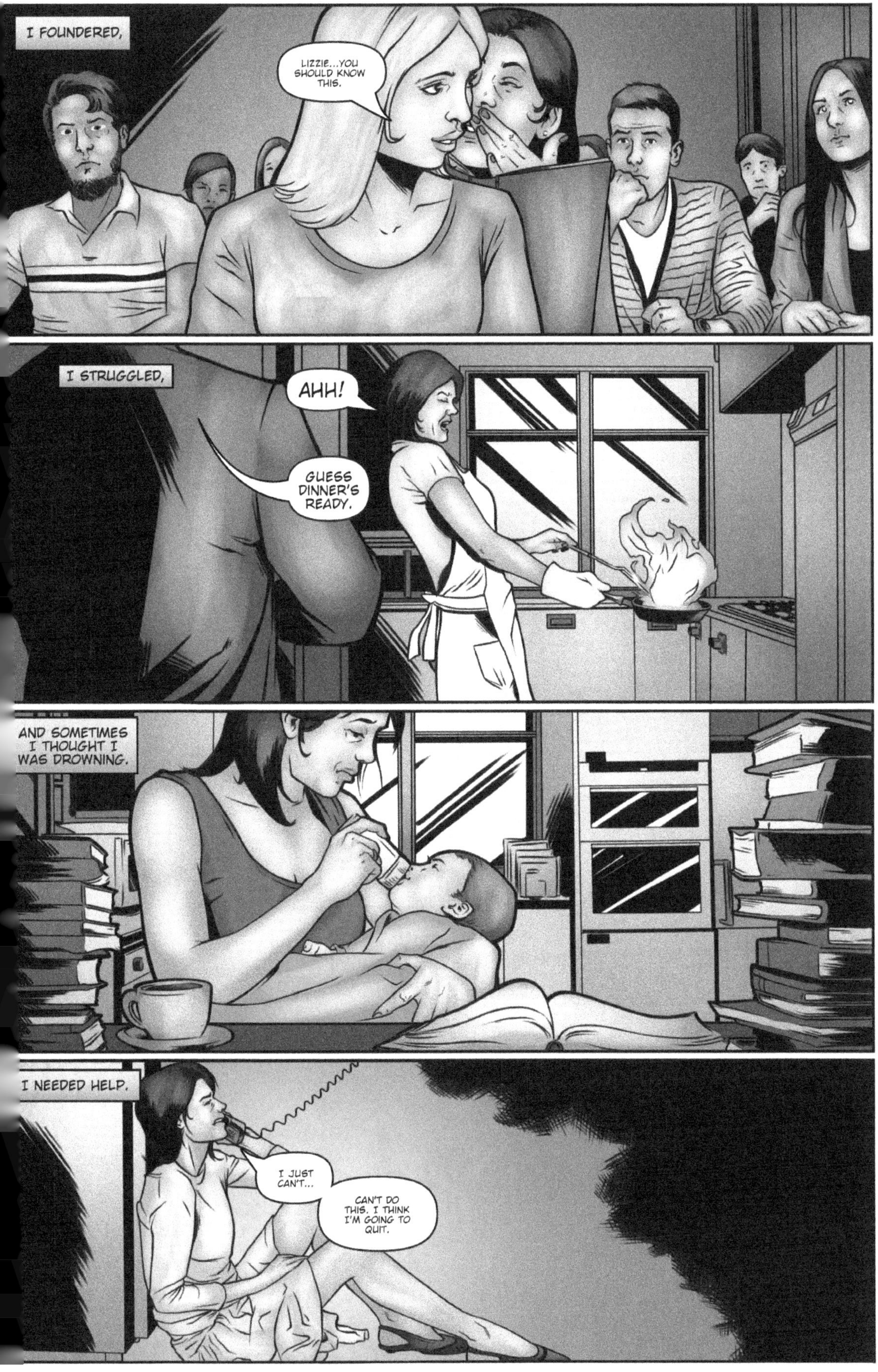
I FOUNDERED,
LIZZIE...YOU SHOULD KNOW THIS.
I STRUGGLED,
AHH!
GUESS DINNER'S READY.
AND SOMETIMES I THOUGHT I WAS DROWNING.
I NEEDED HELP.
I JUST CAN'T...
CAN'T DO THIS. I THINK I'M GOING TO QUIT.

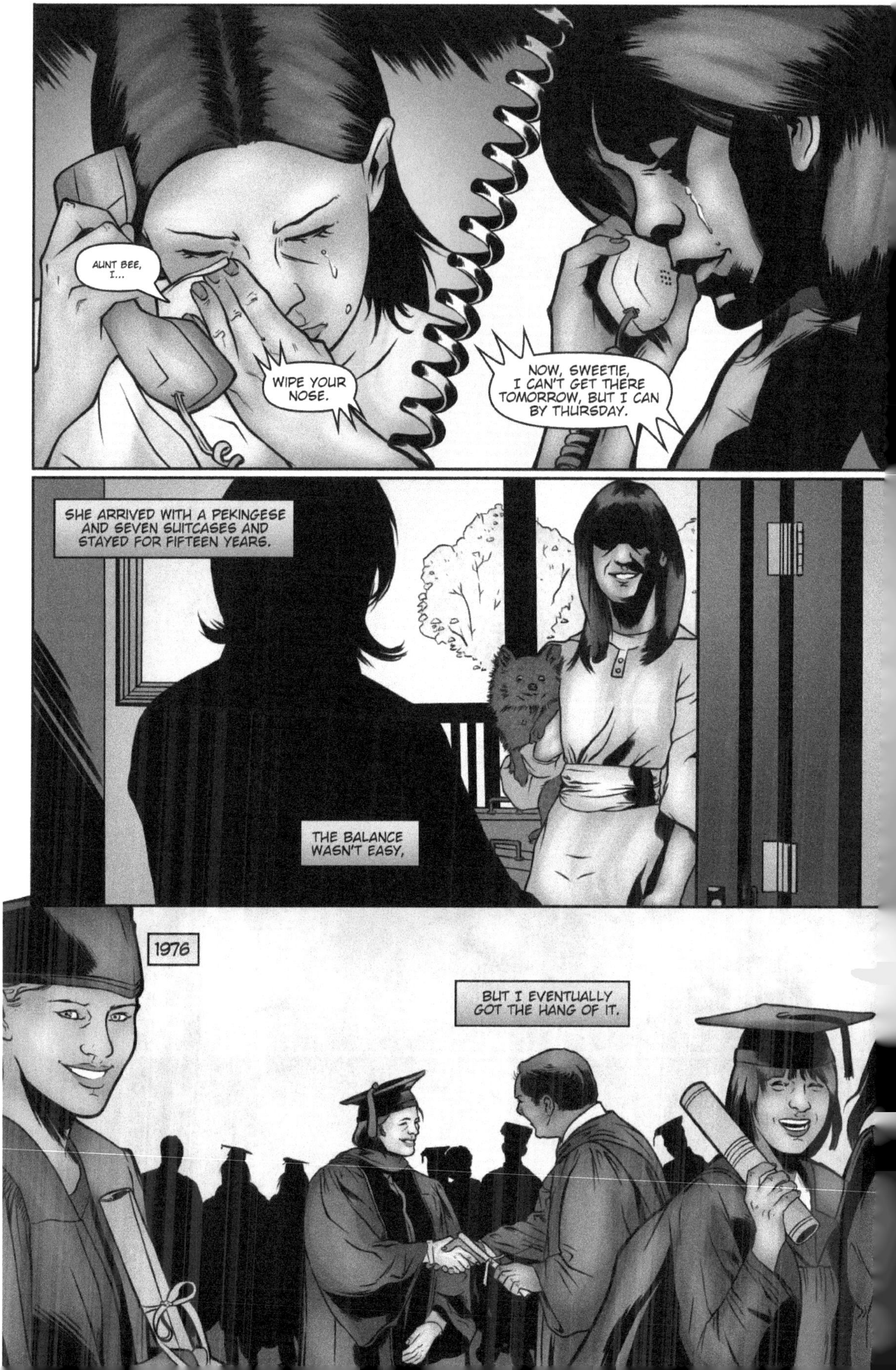
AUNT BEE, I...
WIPE YOUR NOSE.
NOW, SWEETIE, I CAN'T GET THERE TOMORROW, BUT I CAN BY THURSDAY.
SHE ARRIVED WITH A PEKINGESE AND SEVEN SUITCASES AND STAYED FOR FIFTEEN YEARS.
THE BALANCE WASN'T EASY,
1976
BUT I EVENTUALLY GOT THE HANG OF IT.

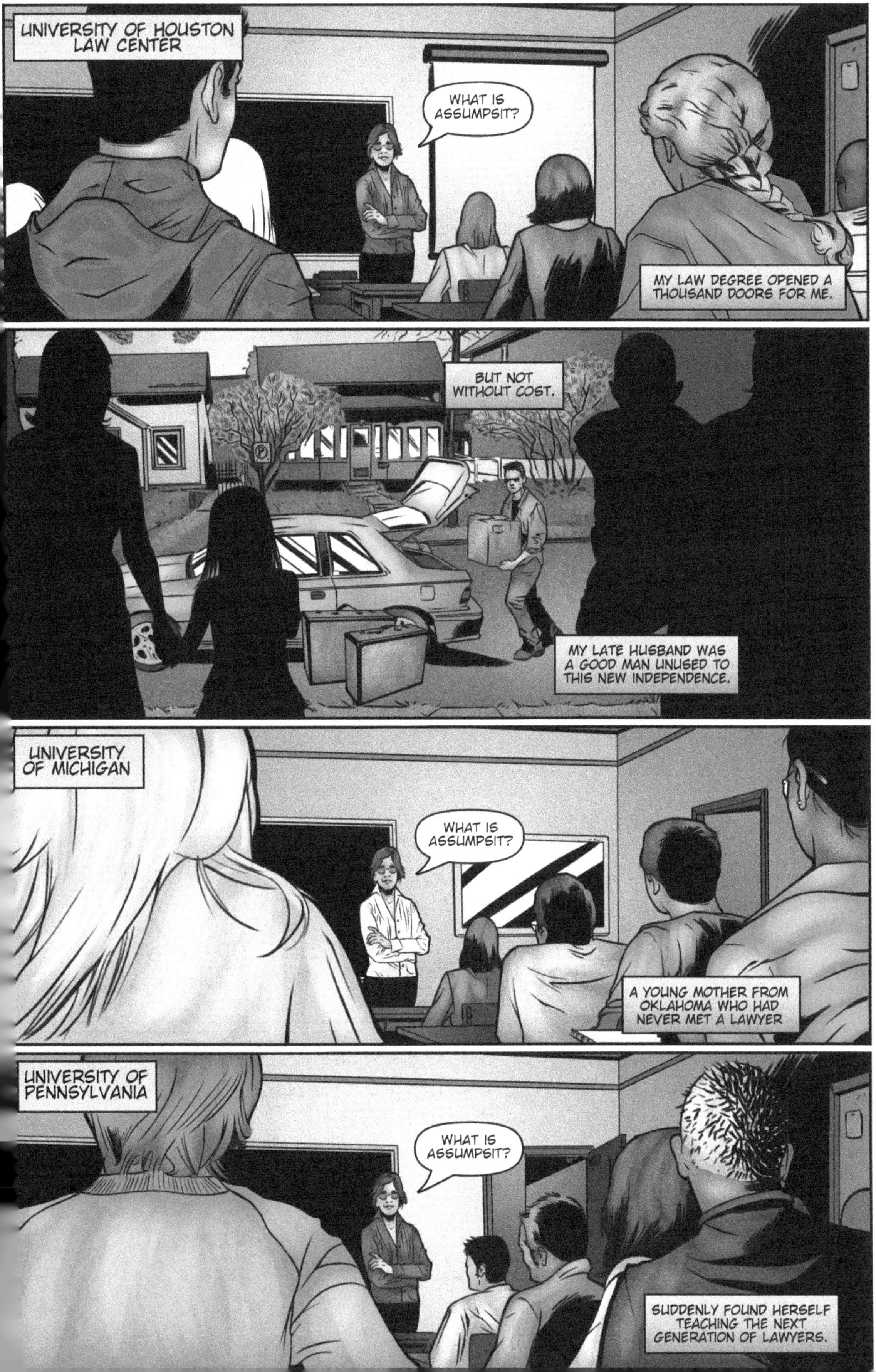
UNIVERSITY OF HOUSTON LAW CENTER
WHAT IS ASSUMPSIT?
MY LAW DEGREE OPENED A THOUSAND DOORS FOR ME.
BUT NOT WITHOUT COST.
MY LATE HUSBAND WAS A GOOD MAN UNUSED TO THIS NEW INDEPENDENCE.
UNIVERSITY OF MICHIGAN
WHAT IS ASSUMPSIT?
A YOUNG MOTHER FROM OKLAHOMA WHO HAD NEVER MET A LAWYER
UNIVERSITY OF PENNSYLVANIA
WHAT IS ASSUMPSIT?
SUDDENLY FOUND HERSELF TEACHING THE NEXT GENERATION OF LAWYERS.

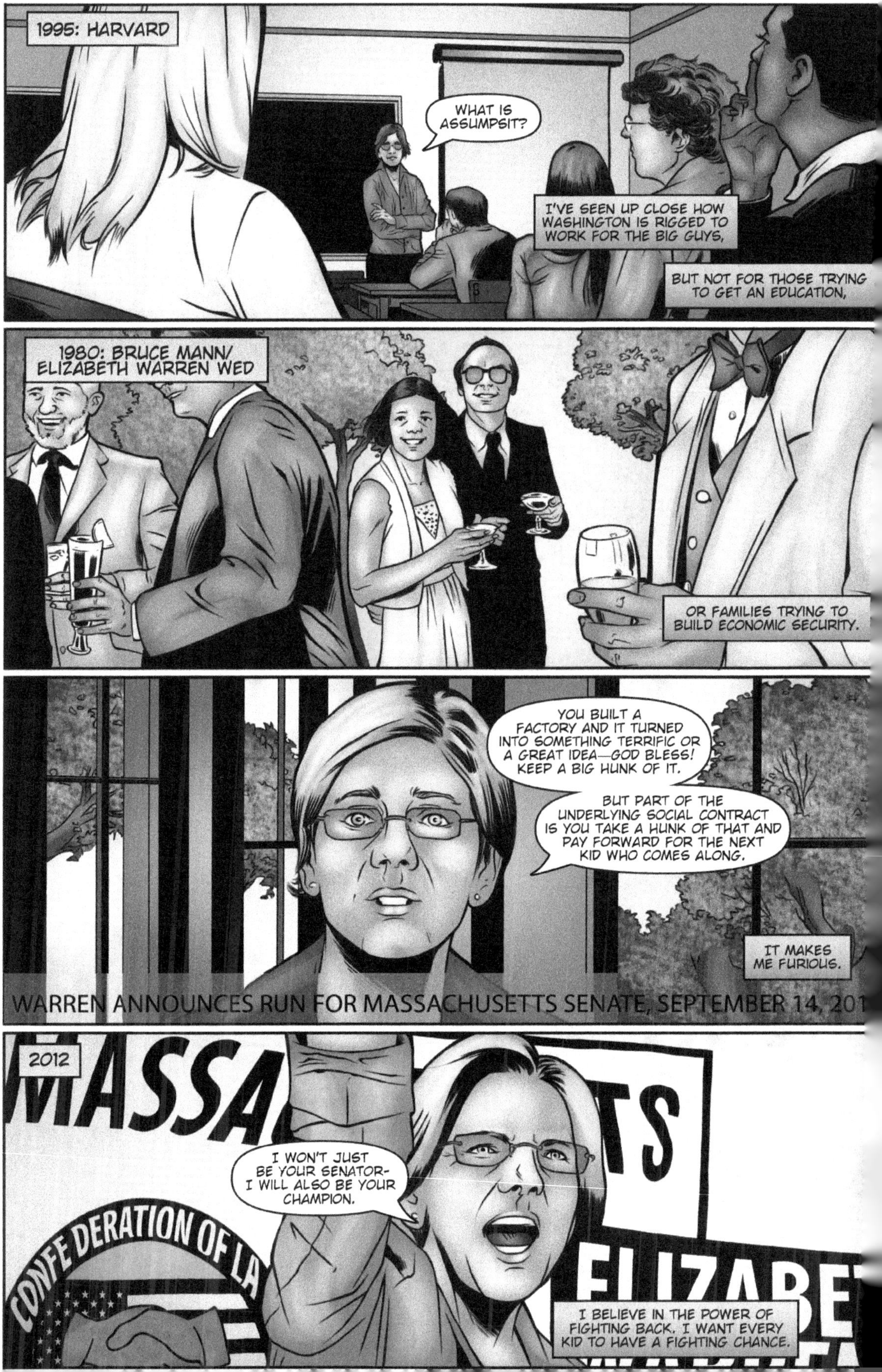
1995: HARVARD
WHAT IS ASSUMPSIT?
I'VE SEEN UP CLOSE HOW WASHINGTON IS RIGGED TO WORK FOR THE BIG GUYS,
BUT NOT FOR THOSE TRYING TO GET AN EDUCATION,
1980: BRUCE MANN/ ELIZABETH WARREN WED
OR FAMILIES TRYING TO BUILD ECONOMIC SECURITY.
YOU BUILT A FACTORY AND IT TURNED INTO SOMETHING TERRIFIC OR A GREAT IDEA—GOD BLESS! KEEP A BIG HUNK OF IT.
BUT PART OF THE UNDERLYING SOCIAL CONTRACT IS YOU TAKE A HUNK OF THAT AND PAY FORWARD FOR THE NEXT KID WHO COMES ALONG.
IT MAKES ME FURIOUS.
WARREN ANNOUNCES RUN FOR MASSACHUSETTS SENATE, SEPTEMBER 14, 201
2012
MASSA
TS
I WON'T JUST BE YOUR SENATOR- I WILL ALSO BE YOUR CHAMPION.
CONFE DERATION OF LA
I BELIEVE IN THE POWER OF FIGHTING BACK. I WANT EVERY KID TO HAVE A FIGHTING CHANCE.

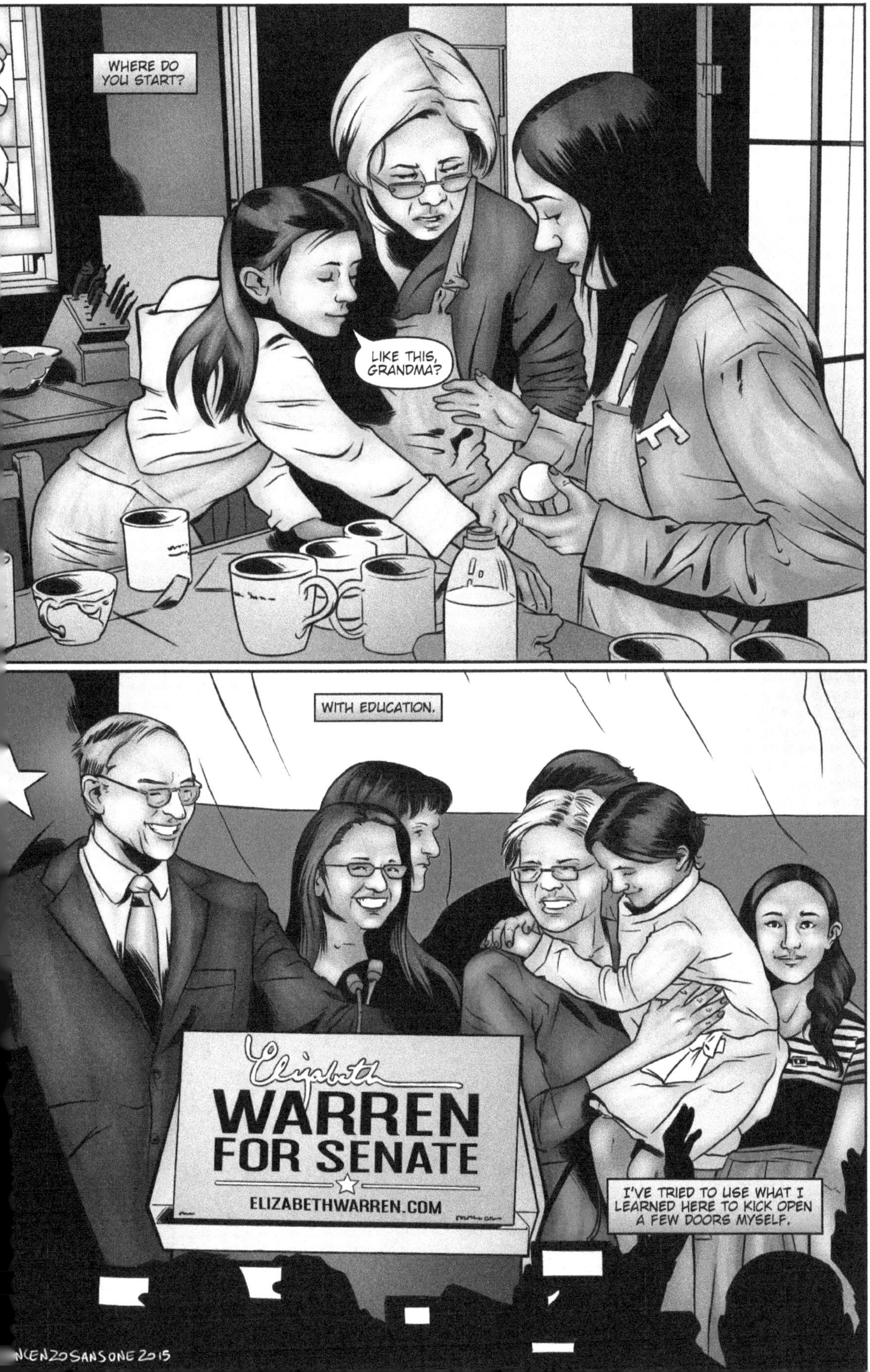
WHERE DO YOU START?
LIKE THIS, GRANDMA?
WITH EDUCATION.
Elizabeth
WARREN FOR SENATE
ELIZABETHWARREN.COM
I'VE TRIED TO USE WHAT I LEARNED HERE TO KICK OPEN A FEW DOORS MYSELF.
NCENZOSANSONE 2015

# CHAPTER TWO

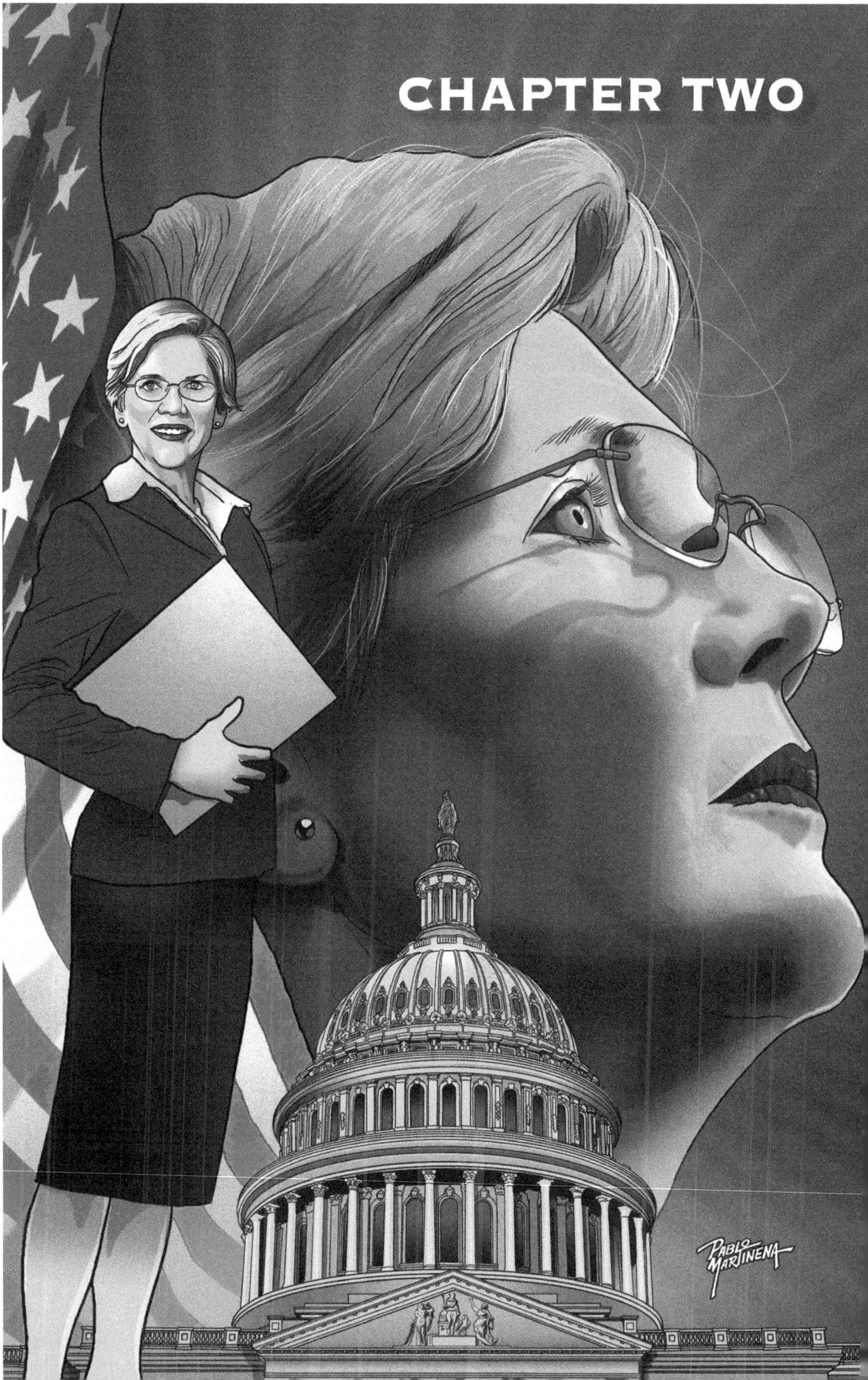
PABLO MARTINENA

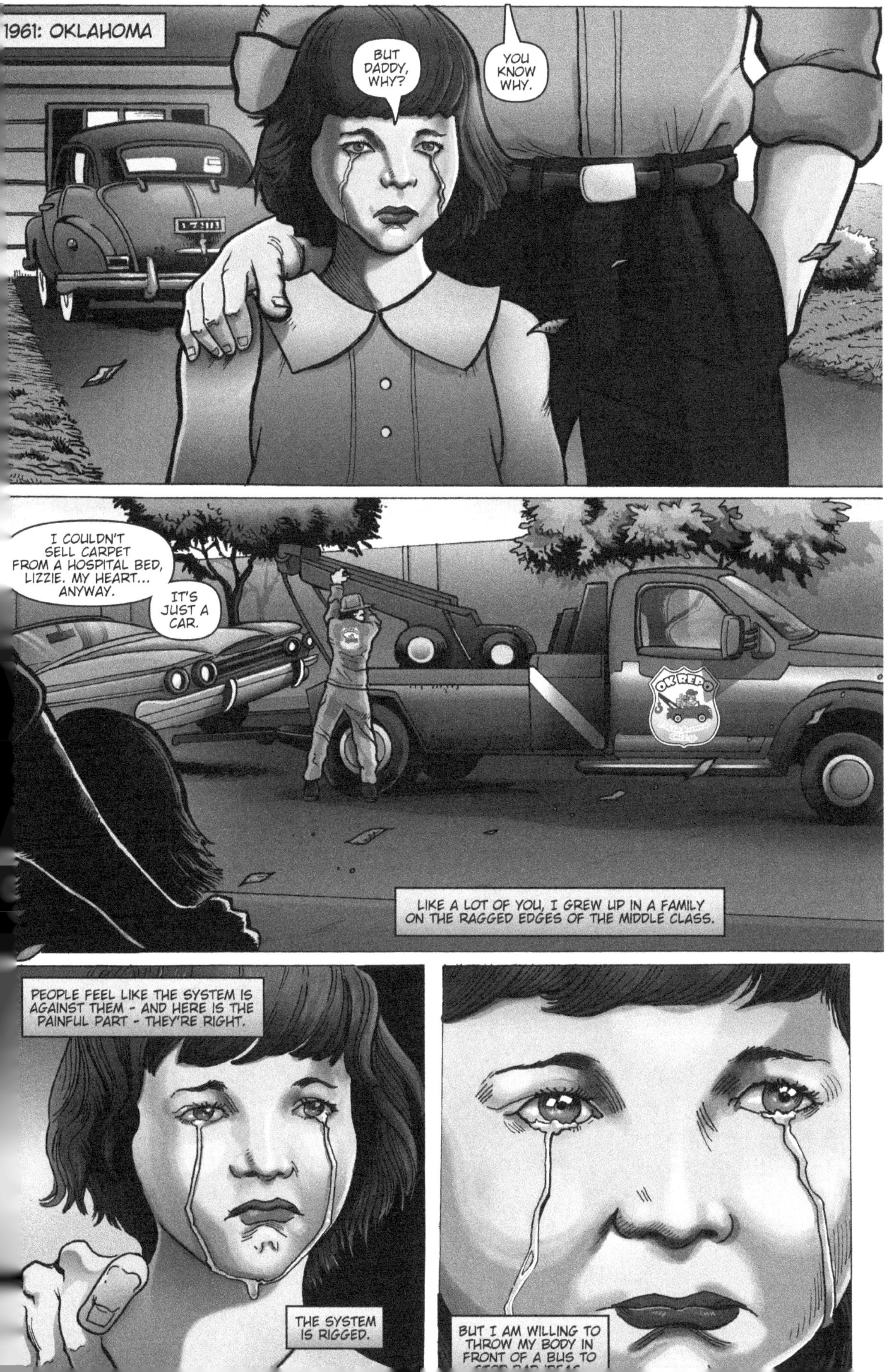
1961: OKLAHOMA
BUT DADDY, WHY?
YOU KNOW WHY.
I COULDN'T SELL CARPET FROM A HOSPITAL BED, LIZZIE. MY HEART... ANYWAY.
IT'S JUST A CAR.
OK REPO
LIKE A LOT OF YOU, I GREW UP IN A FAMILY ON THE RAGGED EDGES OF THE MIDDLE CLASS.
PEOPLE FEEL LIKE THE SYSTEM IS AGAINST THEM - AND HERE IS THE PAINFUL PART - THEY'RE RIGHT.
THE SYSTEM IS RIGGED.
BUT I AM WILLING TO THROW MY BODY IN FRONT OF A BUS TO

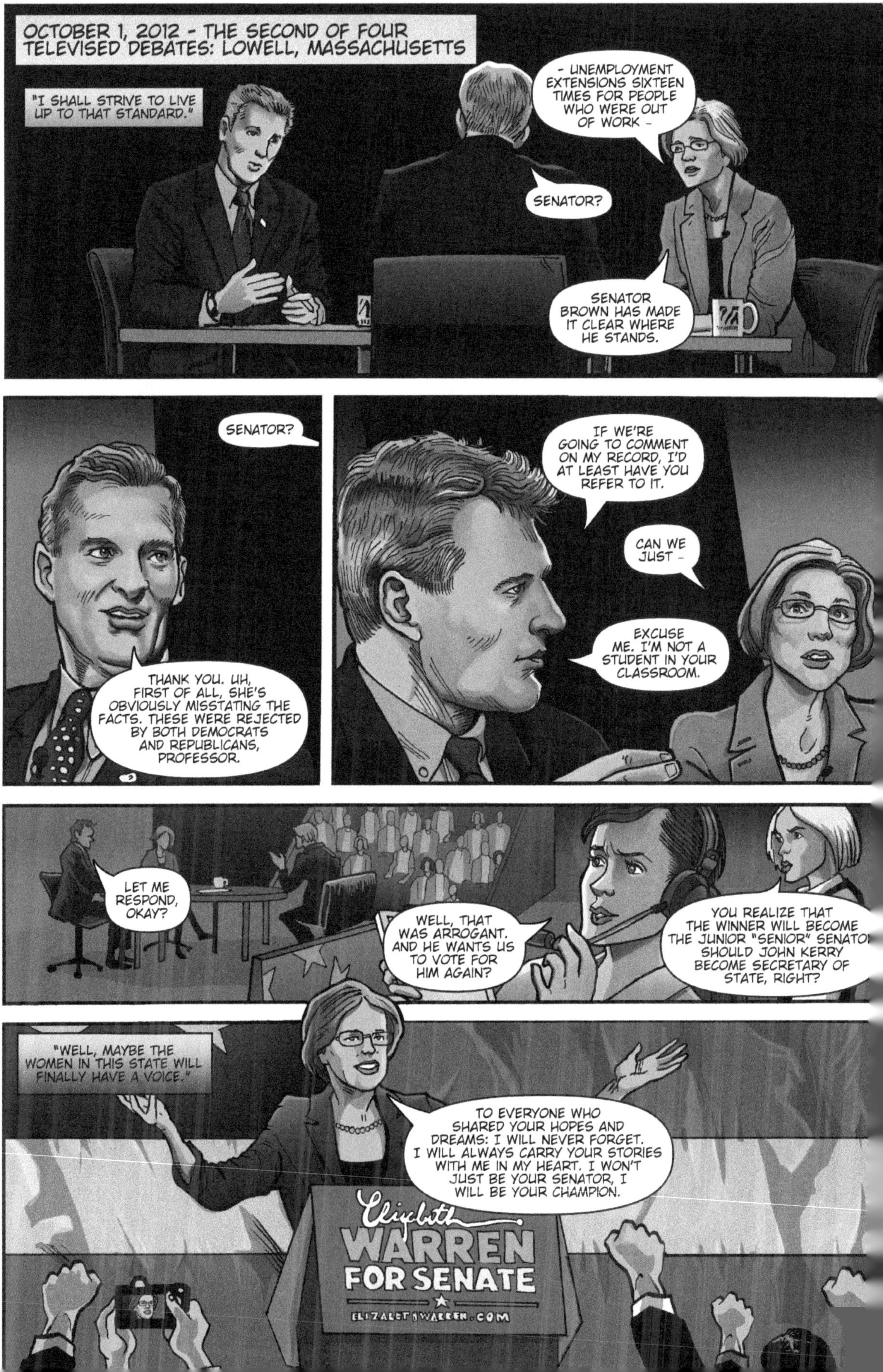
OCTOBER 1, 2012 - THE SECOND OF FOUR TELEVISED DEBATES: LOWELL, MASSACHUSETTS
"I SHALL STRIVE TO LIVE UP TO THAT STANDARD."
- UNEMPLOYMENT EXTENSIONS SIXTEEN TIMES FOR PEOPLE WHO WERE OUT OF WORK -
SENATOR?
SENATOR BROWN HAS MADE IT CLEAR WHERE HE STANDS.
SENATOR?
THANK YOU. UH, FIRST OF ALL, SHE'S OBVIOUSLY MISSTATING THE FACTS. THESE WERE REJECTED BY BOTH DEMOCRATS AND REPUBLICANS, PROFESSOR.
IF WE'RE GOING TO COMMENT ON MY RECORD, I'D AT LEAST HAVE YOU REFER TO IT.
CAN WE JUST -
EXCUSE ME. I'M NOT A STUDENT IN YOUR CLASSROOM.
LET ME RESPOND, OKAY?
WELL, THAT WAS ARROGANT. AND HE WANTS US TO VOTE FOR HIM AGAIN?
YOU REALIZE THAT THE WINNER WILL BECOME THE JUNIOR "SENIOR" SENATOR SHOULD JOHN KERRY BECOME SECRETARY OF STATE, RIGHT?
"WELL, MAYBE THE WOMEN IN THIS STATE WILL FINALLY HAVE A VOICE."
TO EVERYONE WHO SHARED YOUR HOPES AND DREAMS: I WILL NEVER FORGET. I WILL ALWAYS CARRY YOUR STORIES WITH ME IN MY HEART. I WON'T JUST BE YOUR SENATOR, I WILL BE YOUR CHAMPION.
Elizabeth
WARREN
FOR SENATE
ELIZABETHWARREN.COM

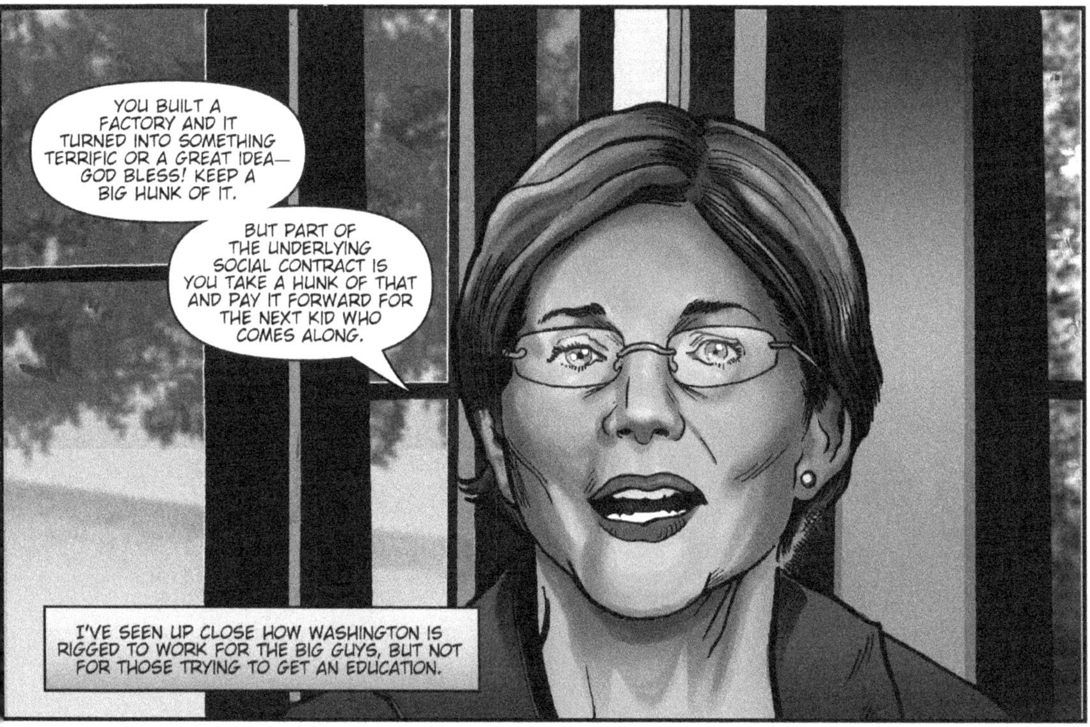
YOU BUILT A FACTORY AND IT TURNED INTO SOMETHING TERRIFIC OR A GREAT IDEA— GOD BLESS! KEEP A BIG HUNK OF IT.
BUT PART OF THE UNDERLYING SOCIAL CONTRACT IS YOU TAKE A HUNK OF THAT AND PAY IT FORWARD FOR THE NEXT KID WHO COMES ALONG.
I'VE SEEN UP CLOSE HOW WASHINGTON IS RIGGED TO WORK FOR THE BIG GUYS, BUT NOT FOR THOSE TRYING TO GET AN EDUCATION.

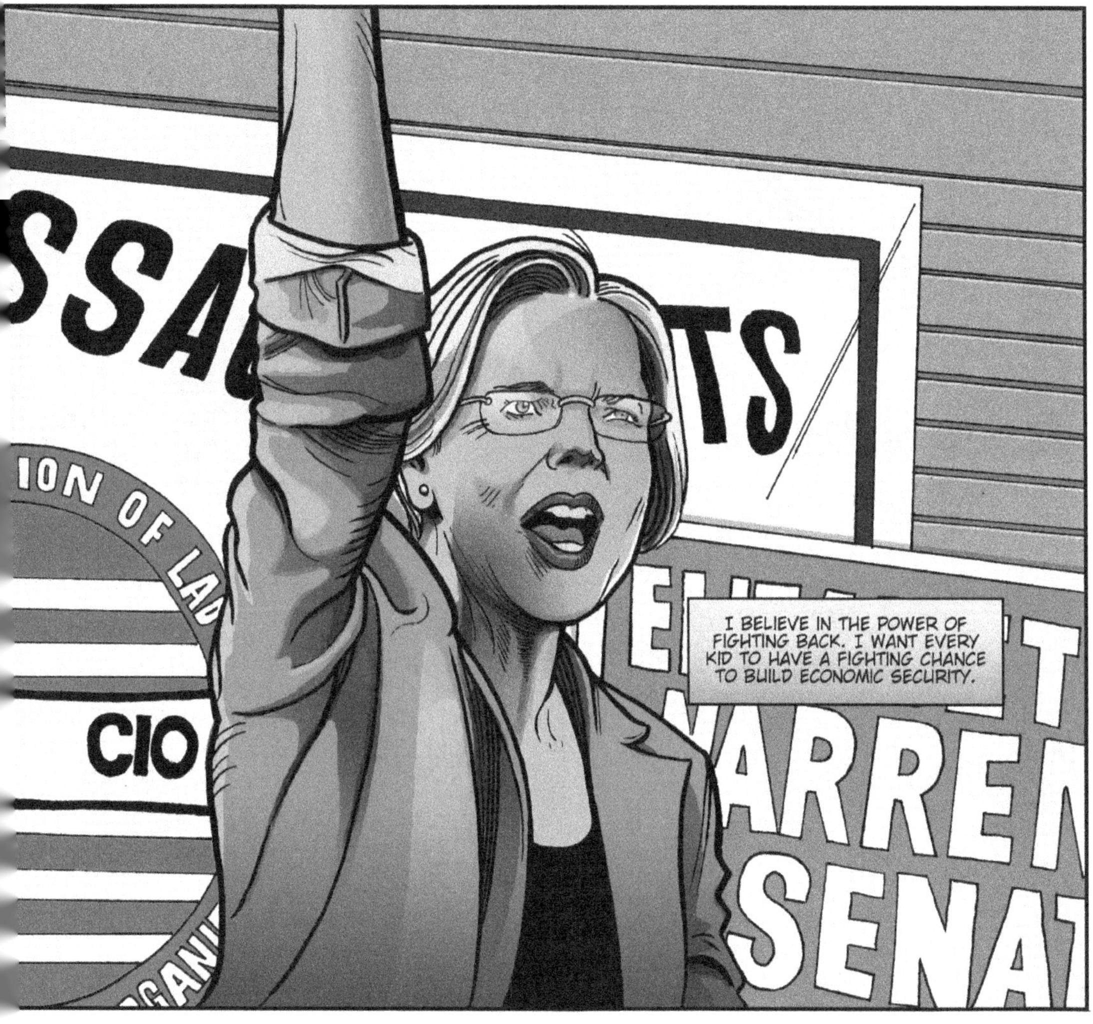
I BELIEVE IN THE POWER OF FIGHTING BACK. I WANT EVERY KID TO HAVE A FIGHTING CHANCE TO BUILD ECONOMIC SECURITY.
CIO

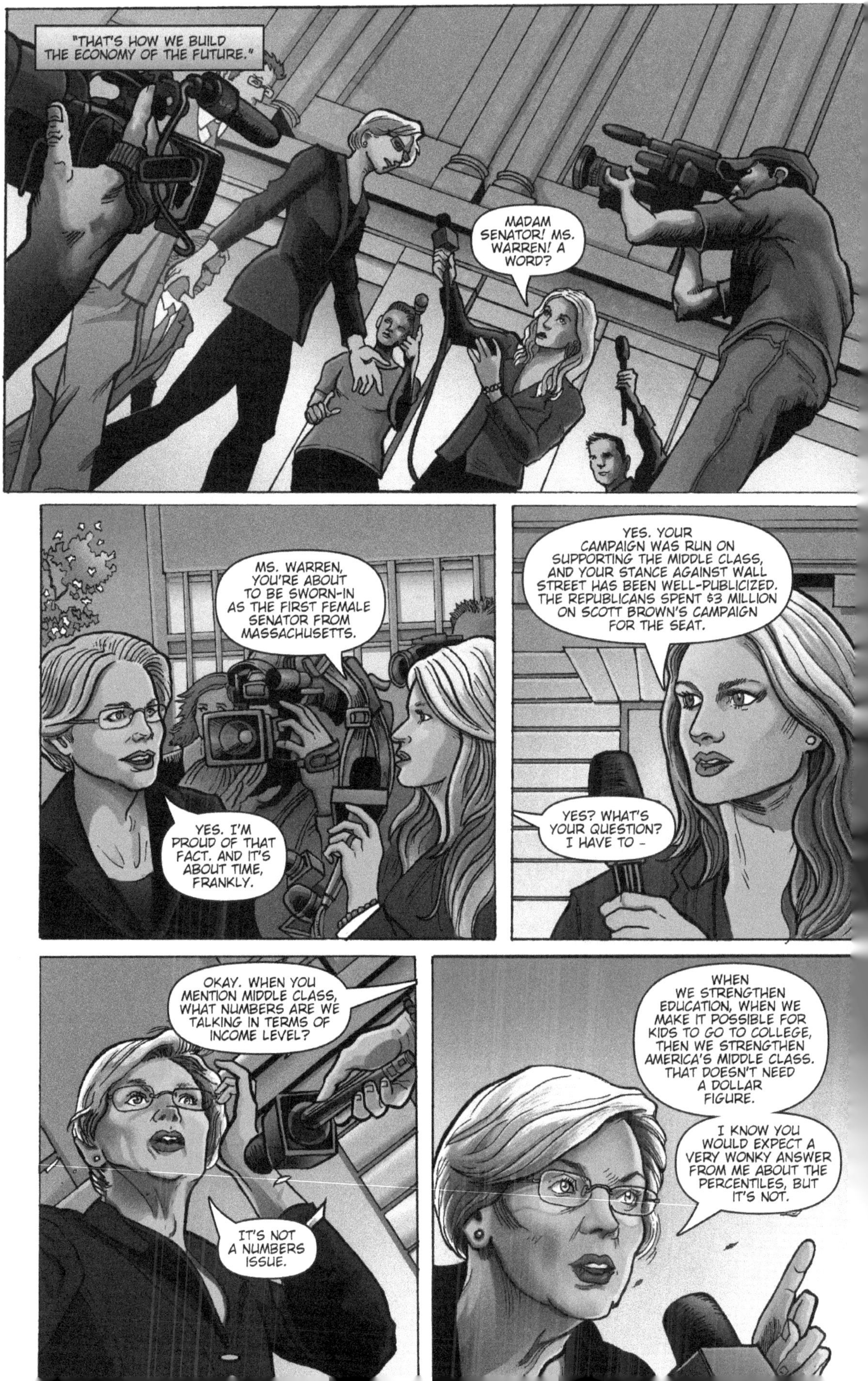
"THAT'S HOW WE BUILD THE ECONOMY OF THE FUTURE."
MADAM SENATOR! MS. WARREN! A WORD?
MS. WARREN, YOU'RE ABOUT TO BE SWORN-IN AS THE FIRST FEMALE SENATOR FROM MASSACHUSETTS.
YES. I'M PROUD OF THAT FACT. AND IT'S ABOUT TIME, FRANKLY.
YES. YOUR CAMPAIGN WAS RUN ON SUPPORTING THE MIDDLE CLASS, AND YOUR STANCE AGAINST WALL STREET HAS BEEN WELL-PUBLICIZED. THE REPUBLICANS SPENT $3 MILLION ON SCOTT BROWN'S CAMPAIGN FOR THE SEAT.
YES? WHAT'S YOUR QUESTION? I HAVE TO -
OKAY. WHEN YOU MENTION MIDDLE CLASS, WHAT NUMBERS ARE WE TALKING IN TERMS OF INCOME LEVEL?
IT'S NOT A NUMBERS ISSUE.
WHEN WE STRENGTHEN EDUCATION, WHEN WE MAKE IT POSSIBLE FOR KIDS TO GO TO COLLEGE, THEN WE STRENGTHEN AMERICA'S MIDDLE CLASS. THAT DOESN'T NEED A DOLLAR FIGURE.
I KNOW YOU WOULD EXPECT A VERY WONKY ANSWER FROM ME ABOUT THE PERCENTILES, BUT IT'S NOT.

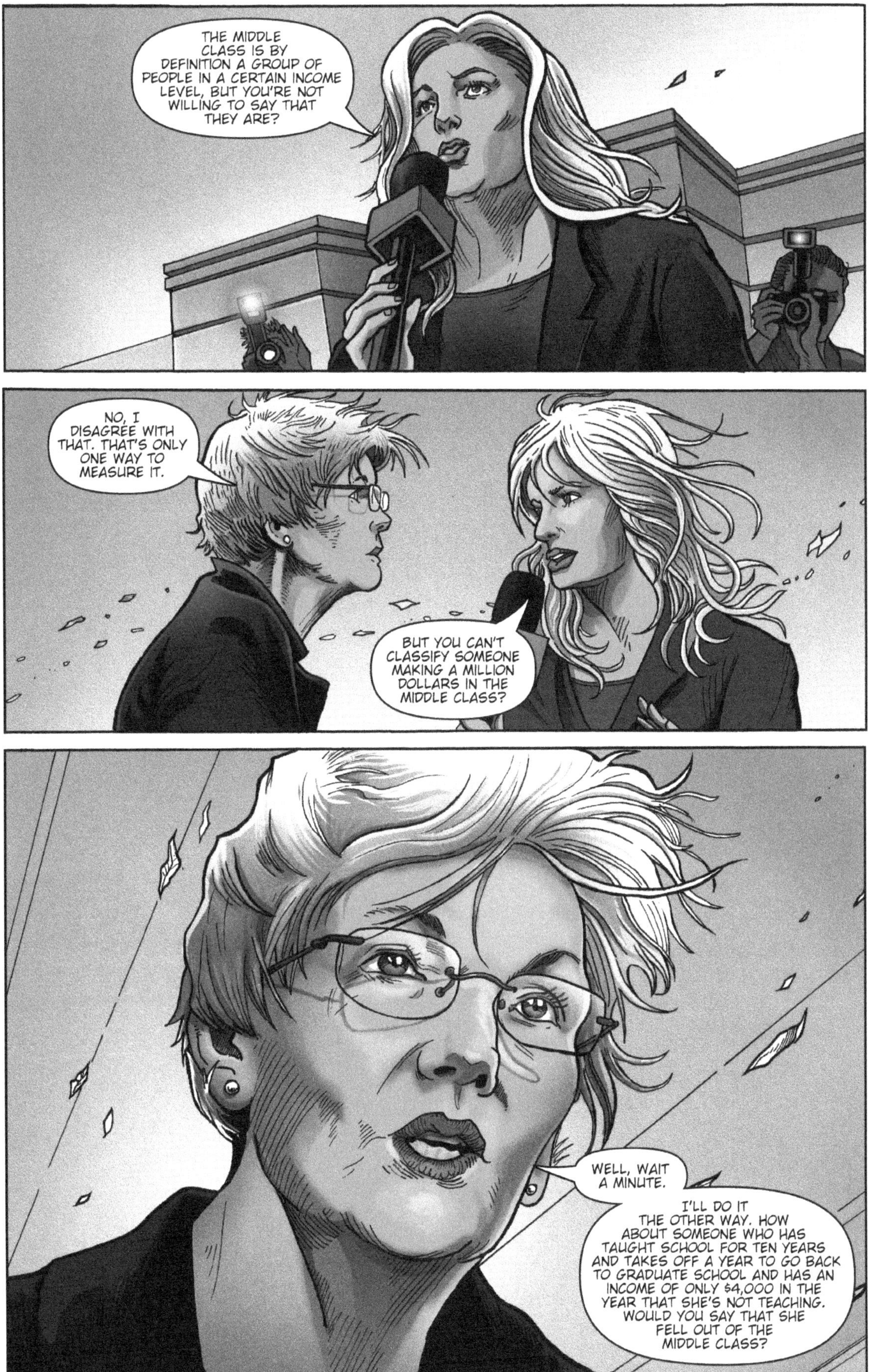
THE MIDDLE CLASS IS BY DEFINITION A GROUP OF PEOPLE IN A CERTAIN INCOME LEVEL, BUT YOU'RE NOT WILLING TO SAY THAT THEY ARE?
NO, I DISAGREE WITH THAT. THAT'S ONLY ONE WAY TO MEASURE IT.
BUT YOU CAN'T CLASSIFY SOMEONE MAKING A MILLION DOLLARS IN THE MIDDLE CLASS?
WELL, WAIT A MINUTE.
I'LL DO IT THE OTHER WAY. HOW ABOUT SOMEONE WHO HAS TAUGHT SCHOOL FOR TEN YEARS AND TAKES OFF A YEAR TO GO BACK TO GRADUATE SCHOOL AND HAS AN INCOME OF ONLY $4,000 IN THE YEAR THAT SHE'S NOT TEACHING. WOULD YOU SAY THAT SHE FELL OUT OF THE MIDDLE CLASS?

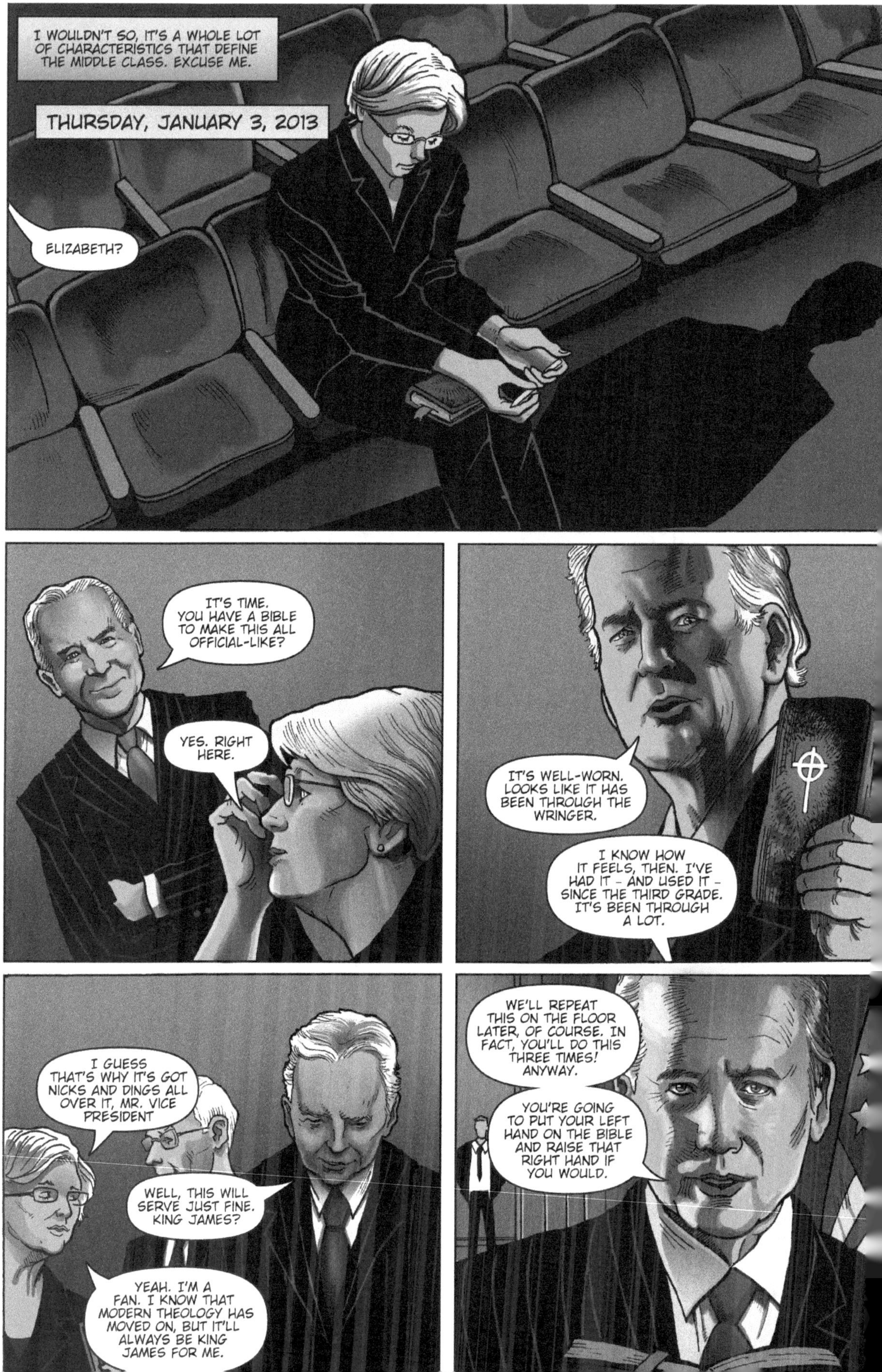

I WOULDN'T SO, IT'S A WHOLE LOT OF CHARACTERISTICS THAT DEFINE THE MIDDLE CLASS. EXCUSE ME.
THURSDAY, JANUARY 3, 2013
ELIZABETH?
IT'S TIME. YOU HAVE A BIBLE TO MAKE THIS ALL OFFICIAL-LIKE?
YES. RIGHT HERE.
IT'S WELL-WORN. LOOKS LIKE IT HAS BEEN THROUGH THE WRINGER.
I KNOW HOW IT FEELS, THEN. I'VE HAD IT - AND USED IT - SINCE THE THIRD GRADE. IT'S BEEN THROUGH A LOT.
I GUESS THAT'S WHY IT'S GOT NICKS AND DINGS ALL OVER IT, MR. VICE PRESIDENT
WELL, THIS WILL SERVE JUST FINE. KING JAMES?
YEAH. I'M A FAN. I KNOW THAT MODERN THEOLOGY HAS MOVED ON, BUT IT'LL ALWAYS BE KING JAMES FOR ME.
WE'LL REPEAT THIS ON THE FLOOR LATER, OF COURSE. IN FACT, YOU'LL DO THIS THREE TIMES! ANYWAY.
YOU'RE GOING TO PUT YOUR LEFT HAND ON THE BIBLE AND RAISE THAT RIGHT HAND IF YOU WOULD.

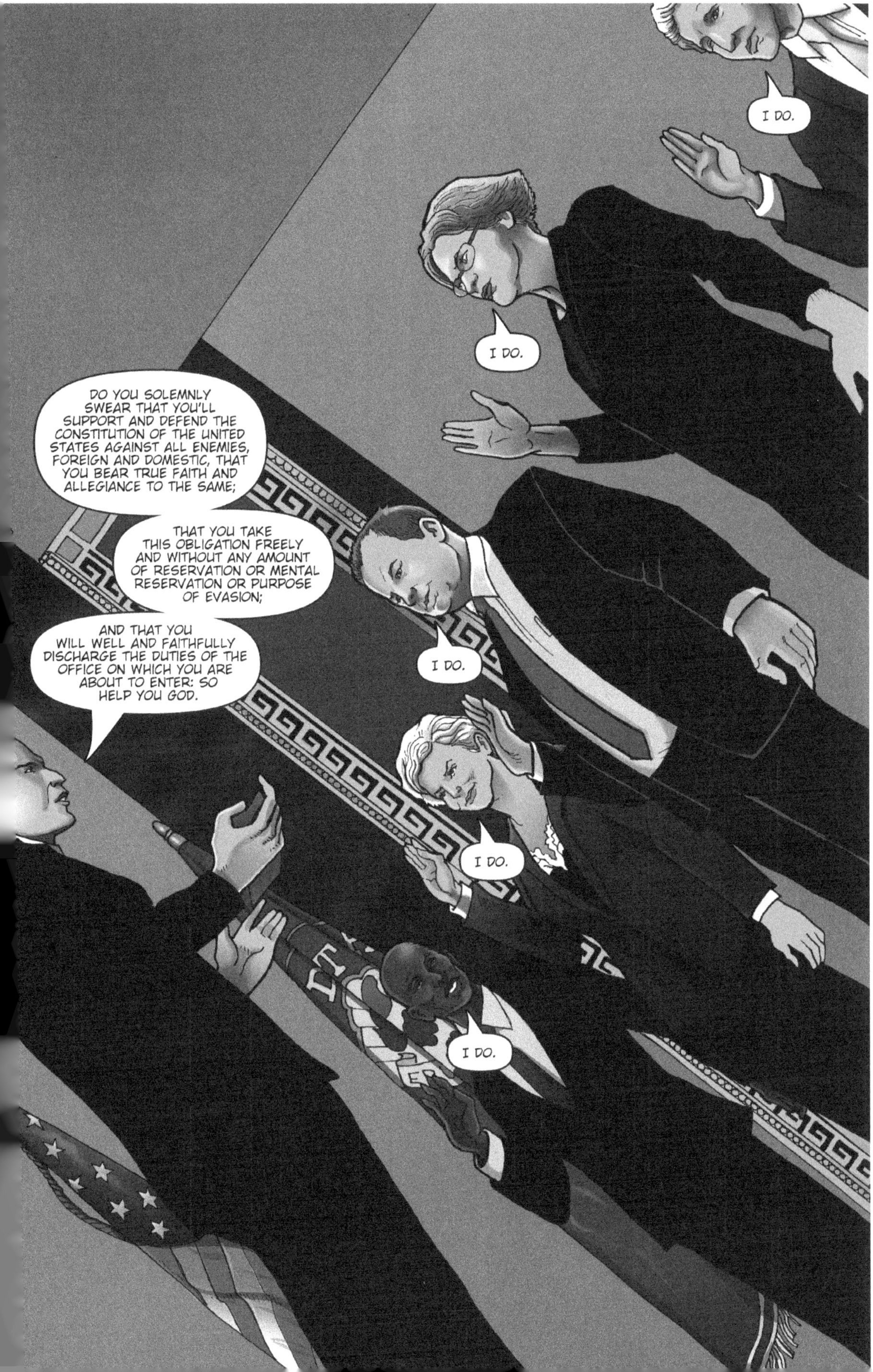
I DO.
I DO.
DO YOU SOLEMNLY SWEAR THAT YOU'LL SUPPORT AND DEFEND THE CONSTITUTION OF THE UNITED STATES AGAINST ALL ENEMIES, FOREIGN AND DOMESTIC, THAT YOU BEAR TRUE FAITH AND ALLEGIANCE TO THE SAME;
THAT YOU TAKE THIS OBLIGATION FREELY AND WITHOUT ANY AMOUNT OF RESERVATION OR MENTAL RESERVATION OR PURPOSE OF EVASION;
AND THAT YOU WILL WELL AND FAITHFULLY DISCHARGE THE DUTIES OF THE OFFICE ON WHICH YOU ARE ABOUT TO ENTER: SO HELP YOU GOD.
I DO.
I DO.
I DO.

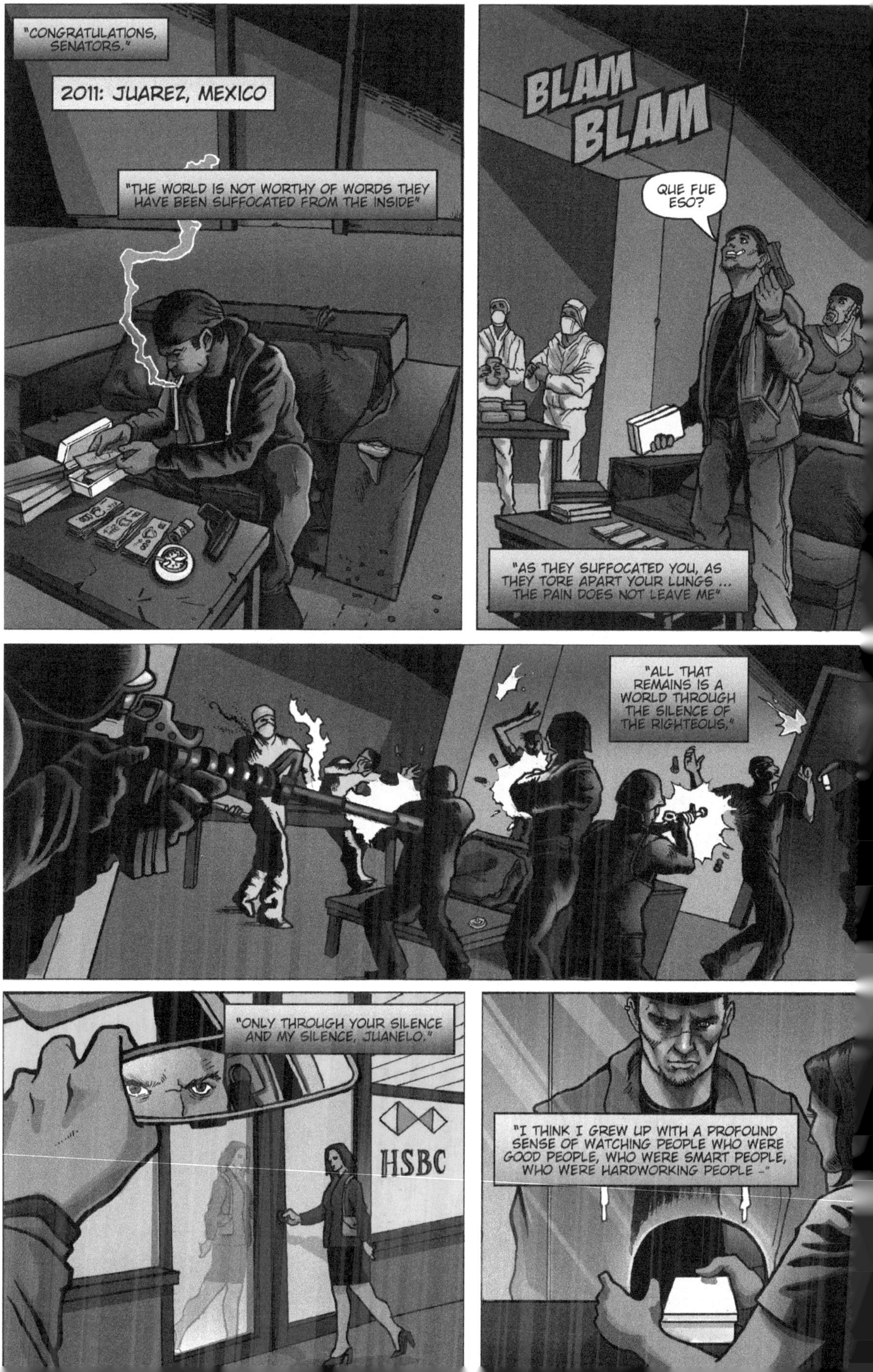
"CONGRATULATIONS, SENATORS."
2011: JUAREZ, MEXICO
"THE WORLD IS NOT WORTHY OF WORDS THEY HAVE BEEN SUFFOCATED FROM THE INSIDE"
BLAM BLAM
QUE FUE ESO?
"AS THEY SUFFOCATED YOU, AS THEY TORE APART YOUR LUNGS ... THE PAIN DOES NOT LEAVE ME"
"ALL THAT REMAINS IS A WORLD THROUGH THE SILENCE OF THE RIGHTEOUS,"
"ONLY THROUGH YOUR SILENCE AND MY SILENCE, JUANELO."
HSBC
"I THINK I GREW UP WITH A PROFOUND SENSE OF WATCHING PEOPLE WHO WERE GOOD PEOPLE, WHO WERE SMART PEOPLE, WHO WERE HARDWORKING PEOPLE –"

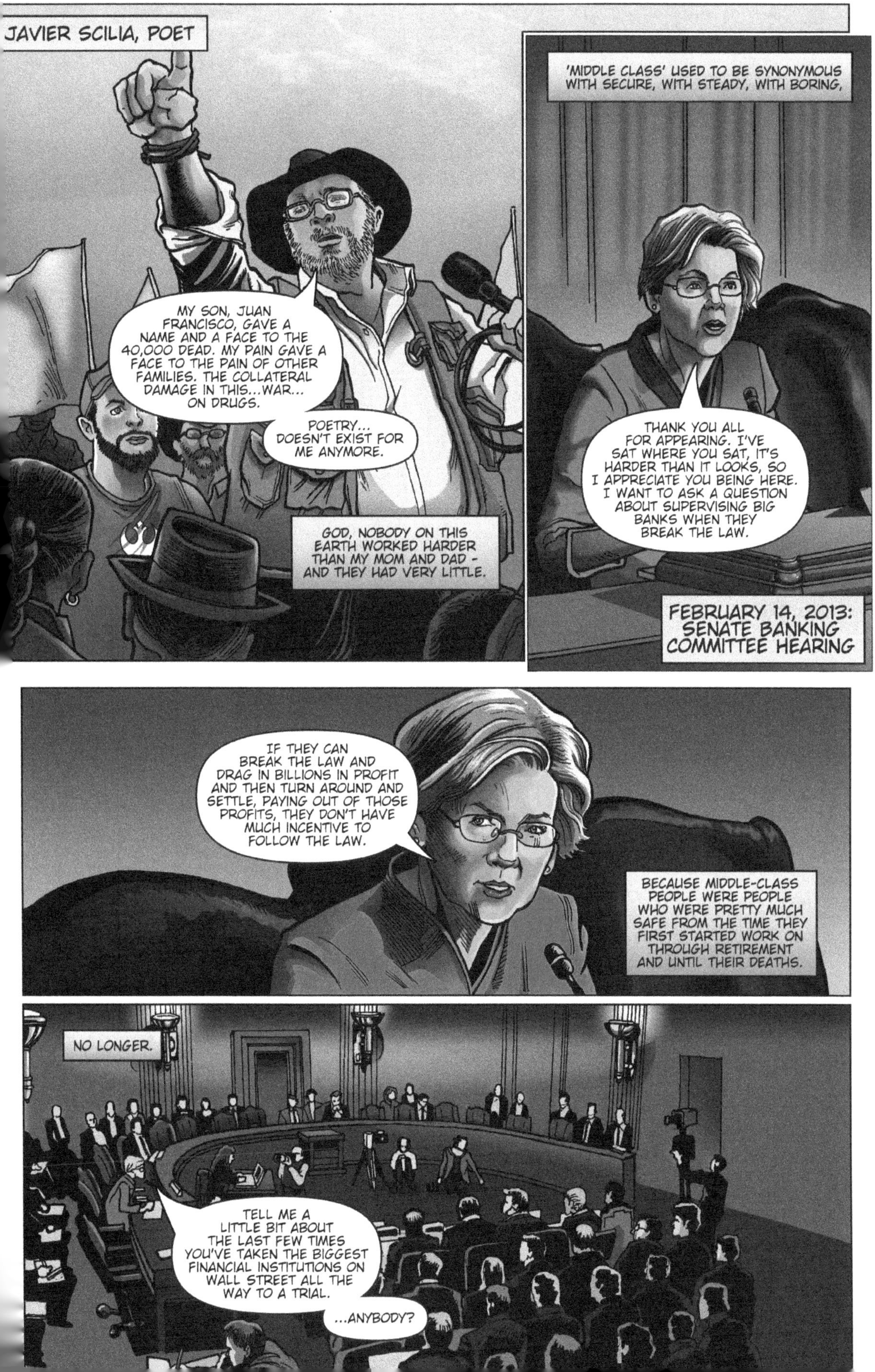
JAVIER SCILIA, POET
MY SON, JUAN FRANCISCO, GAVE A NAME AND A FACE TO THE 40,000 DEAD. MY PAIN GAVE A FACE TO THE PAIN OF OTHER FAMILIES. THE COLLATERAL DAMAGE IN THIS...WAR... ON DRUGS.
POETRY... DOESN'T EXIST FOR ME ANYMORE.
GOD, NOBODY ON THIS EARTH WORKED HARDER THAN MY MOM AND DAD - AND THEY HAD VERY LITTLE.
'MIDDLE CLASS' USED TO BE SYNONYMOUS WITH SECURE, WITH STEADY, WITH BORING,
THANK YOU ALL FOR APPEARING. I'VE SAT WHERE YOU SAT, IT'S HARDER THAN IT LOOKS, SO I APPRECIATE YOU BEING HERE. I WANT TO ASK A QUESTION ABOUT SUPERVISING BIG BANKS WHEN THEY BREAK THE LAW.
FEBRUARY 14, 2013: SENATE BANKING COMMITTEE HEARING
IF THEY CAN BREAK THE LAW AND DRAG IN BILLIONS IN PROFIT AND THEN TURN AROUND AND SETTLE, PAYING OUT OF THOSE PROFITS, THEY DON'T HAVE MUCH INCENTIVE TO FOLLOW THE LAW.
BECAUSE MIDDLE-CLASS PEOPLE WERE PEOPLE WHO WERE PRETTY MUCH SAFE FROM THE TIME THEY FIRST STARTED WORK ON THROUGH RETIREMENT AND UNTIL THEIR DEATHS.
NO LONGER.
TELL ME A LITTLE BIT ABOUT THE LAST FEW TIMES YOU'VE TAKEN THE BIGGEST FINANCIAL INSTITUTIONS ON WALL STREET ALL THE WAY TO A TRIAL.
...ANYBODY?

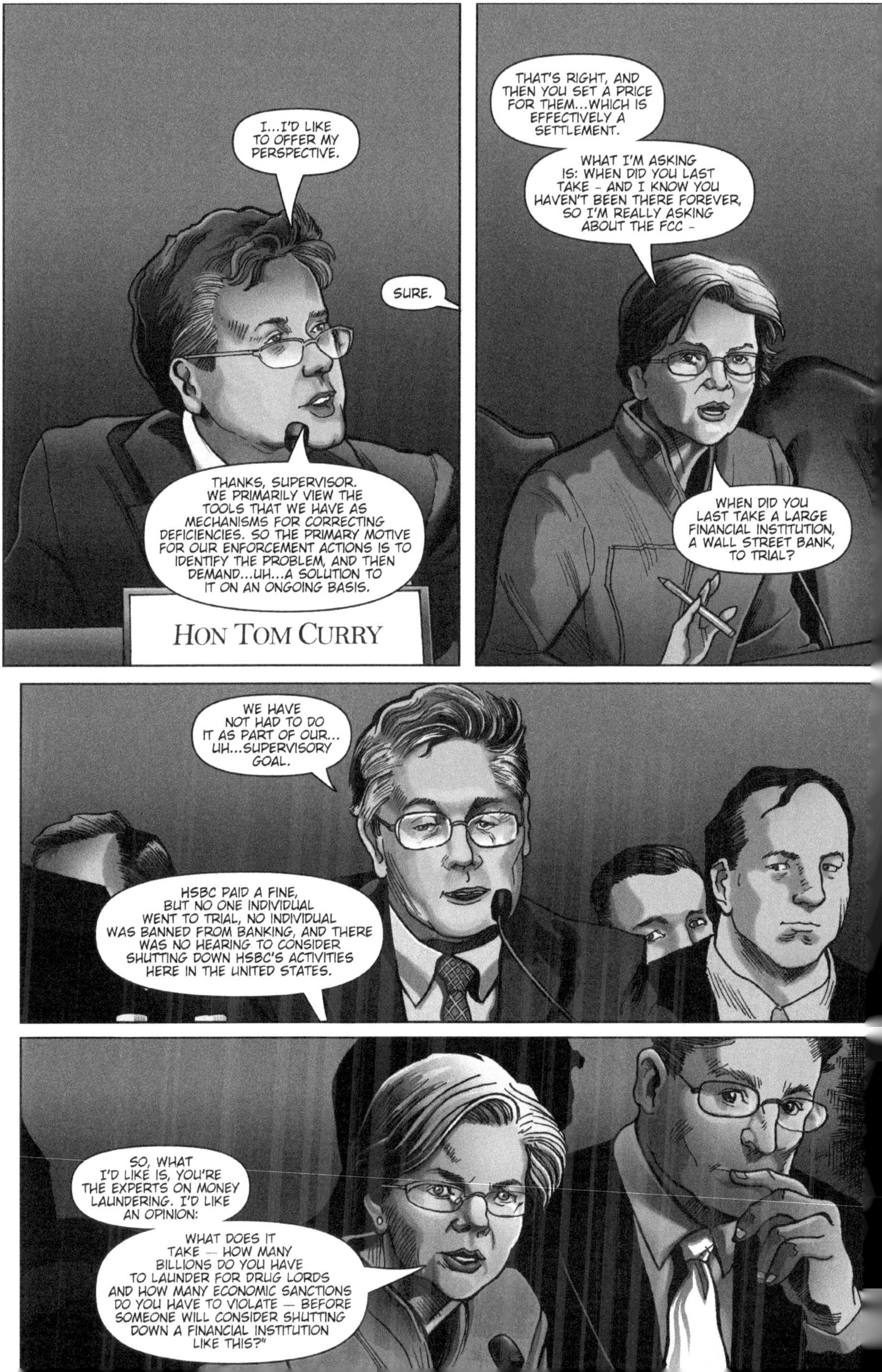
I...I'D LIKE TO OFFER MY PERSPECTIVE.
SURE.
THANKS, SUPERVISOR. WE PRIMARILY VIEW THE TOOLS THAT WE HAVE AS MECHANISMS FOR CORRECTING DEFICIENCIES. SO THE PRIMARY MOTIVE FOR OUR ENFORCEMENT ACTIONS IS TO IDENTIFY THE PROBLEM, AND THEN DEMAND...UH...A SOLUTION TO IT ON AN ONGOING BASIS.
HON TOM CURRY
THAT'S RIGHT, AND THEN YOU SET A PRICE FOR THEM...WHICH IS EFFECTIVELY A SETTLEMENT.
WHAT I'M ASKING IS: WHEN DID YOU LAST TAKE – AND I KNOW YOU HAVEN'T BEEN THERE FOREVER, SO I'M REALLY ASKING ABOUT THE FCC –
WHEN DID YOU LAST TAKE A LARGE FINANCIAL INSTITUTION, A WALL STREET BANK, TO TRIAL?
WE HAVE NOT HAD TO DO IT AS PART OF OUR... UH...SUPERVISORY GOAL.
HSBC PAID A FINE, BUT NO ONE INDIVIDUAL WENT TO TRIAL, NO INDIVIDUAL WAS BANNED FROM BANKING, AND THERE WAS NO HEARING TO CONSIDER SHUTTING DOWN HSBC'S ACTIVITIES HERE IN THE UNITED STATES.
SO, WHAT I'D LIKE IS, YOU'RE THE EXPERTS ON MONEY LAUNDERING. I'D LIKE AN OPINION:
WHAT DOES IT TAKE — HOW MANY BILLIONS DO YOU HAVE TO LAUNDER FOR DRUG LORDS AND HOW MANY ECONOMIC SANCTIONS DO YOU HAVE TO VIOLATE — BEFORE SOMEONE WILL CONSIDER SHUTTING DOWN A FINANCIAL INSTITUTION LIKE THIS?"

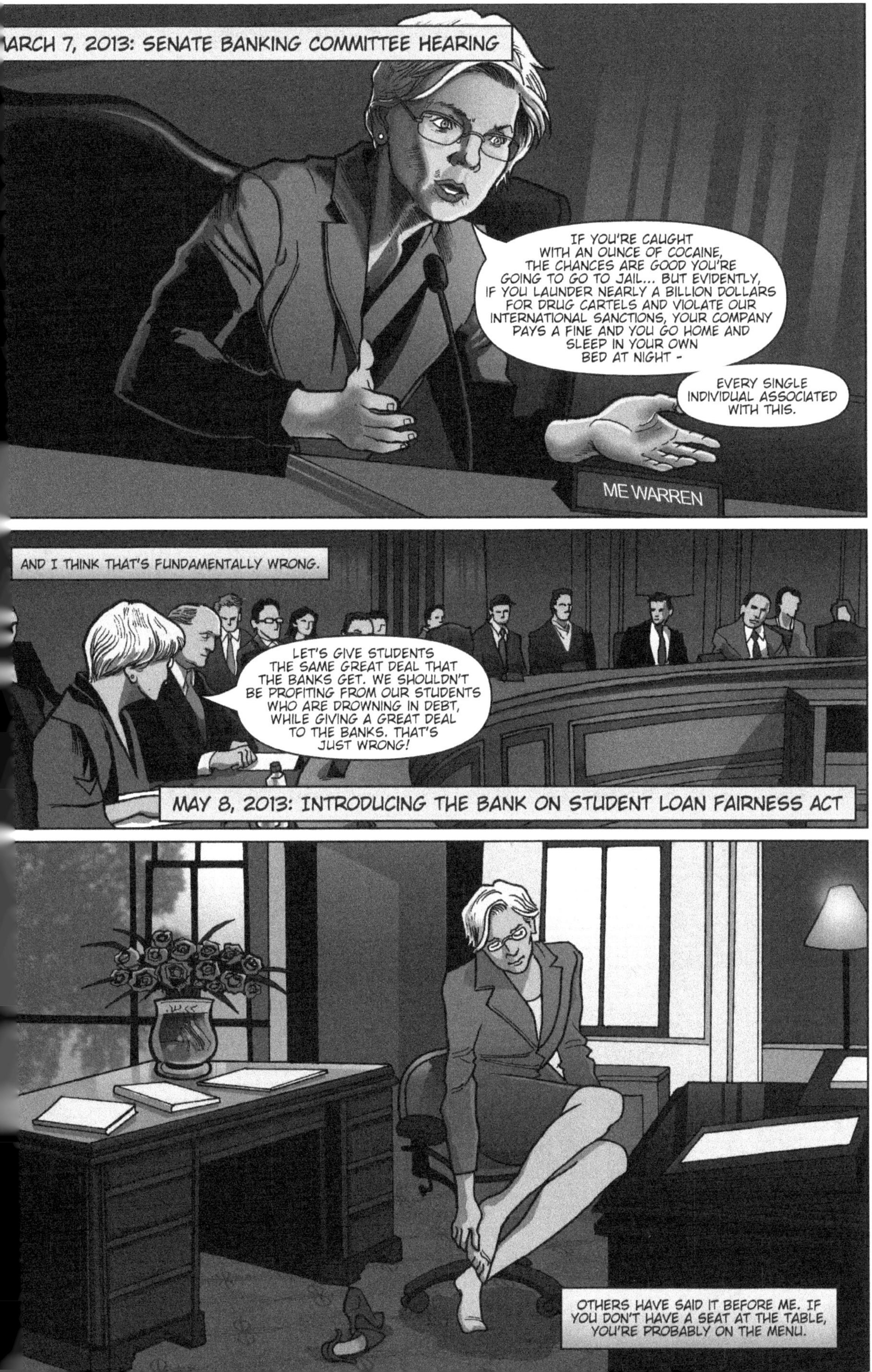

ARCH 7, 2013: SENATE BANKING COMMITTEE HEARING
IF YOU'RE CAUGHT WITH AN OUNCE OF COCAINE, THE CHANCES ARE GOOD YOU'RE GOING TO GO TO JAIL... BUT EVIDENTLY, IF YOU LAUNDER NEARLY A BILLION DOLLARS FOR DRUG CARTELS AND VIOLATE OUR INTERNATIONAL SANCTIONS, YOUR COMPANY PAYS A FINE AND YOU GO HOME AND SLEEP IN YOUR OWN BED AT NIGHT -
EVERY SINGLE INDIVIDUAL ASSOCIATED WITH THIS.
ME WARREN
AND I THINK THAT'S FUNDAMENTALLY WRONG.
LET'S GIVE STUDENTS THE SAME GREAT DEAL THAT THE BANKS GET. WE SHOULDN'T BE PROFITING FROM OUR STUDENTS WHO ARE DROWNING IN DEBT, WHILE GIVING A GREAT DEAL TO THE BANKS. THAT'S JUST WRONG!
MAY 8, 2013: INTRODUCING THE BANK ON STUDENT LOAN FAIRNESS ACT
OTHERS HAVE SAID IT BEFORE ME. IF YOU DON'T HAVE A SEAT AT THE TABLE, YOU'RE PROBABLY ON THE MENU.

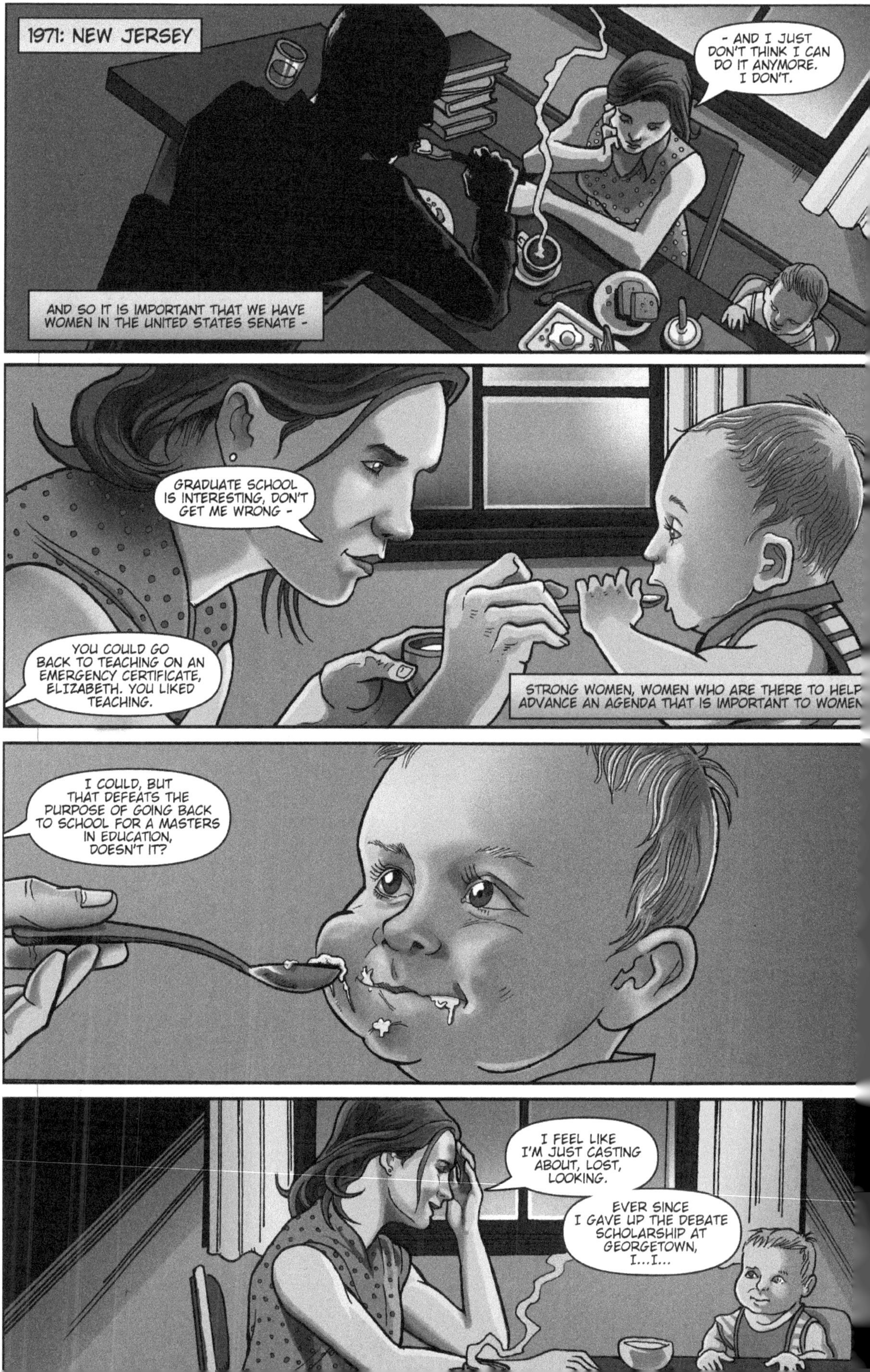
1971: NEW JERSEY
- AND I JUST DON'T THINK I CAN DO IT ANYMORE. I DON'T.
AND SO IT IS IMPORTANT THAT WE HAVE WOMEN IN THE UNITED STATES SENATE -
GRADUATE SCHOOL IS INTERESTING, DON'T GET ME WRONG -
YOU COULD GO BACK TO TEACHING ON AN EMERGENCY CERTIFICATE, ELIZABETH. YOU LIKED TEACHING.
STRONG WOMEN, WOMEN WHO ARE THERE TO HELP ADVANCE AN AGENDA THAT IS IMPORTANT TO WOMEN
I COULD, BUT THAT DEFEATS THE PURPOSE OF GOING BACK TO SCHOOL FOR A MASTERS IN EDUCATION, DOESN'T IT?
I FEEL LIKE I'M JUST CASTING ABOUT, LOST, LOOKING.
EVER SINCE I GAVE UP THE DEBATE SCHOLARSHIP AT GEORGETOWN, I...I...

STAY HOME. WE HAVE A CHILD AND WE'LL HAVE MORE CHILDREN. YOU'LL LOVE THIS.

GOING TO WORK. LOVE YOU.

SLAM!

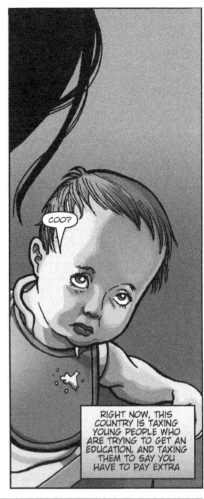

COO?

RIGHT NOW, THIS COUNTRY IS TAXING YOUNG PEOPLE WHO ARE TRYING TO GET AN EDUCATION, AND TAXING THEM TO SAY YOU HAVE TO PAY EXTRA

YOU CAN'T BE SERIOUS, KARL. NOW?

WHY NOT NOW?

(UNLESS YOU ARE BORN INTO A FAMILY WHO CAN JUST WRITE A CHECK FOR COLLEGE)

TWO KIDS, A MORTGAGE...

AND YOU KNOW WHY YOU HAVE TO PAY EXTRA?

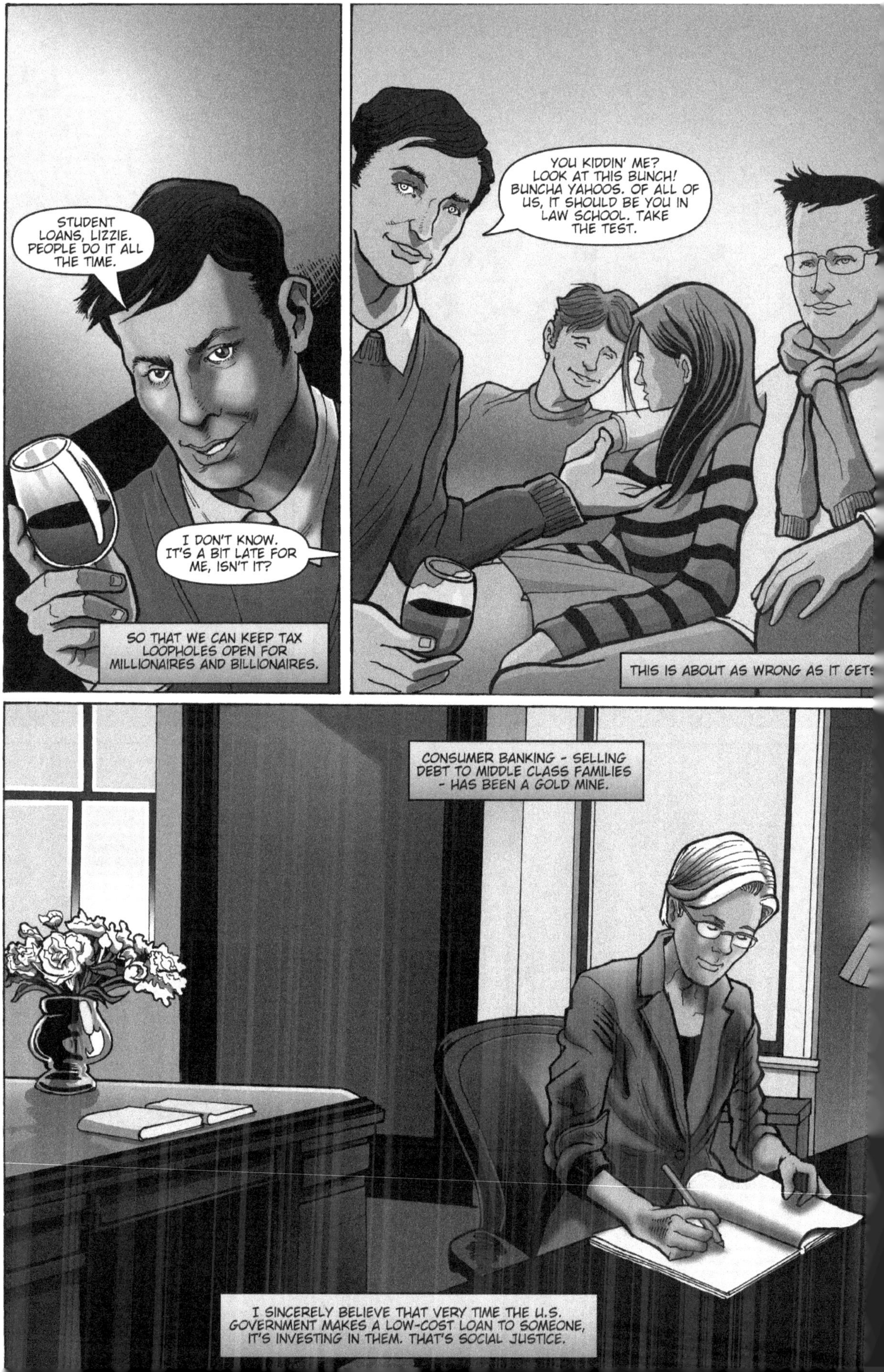
STUDENT LOANS, LIZZIE. PEOPLE DO IT ALL THE TIME.
I DON'T KNOW. IT'S A BIT LATE FOR ME, ISN'T IT?
SO THAT WE CAN KEEP TAX LOOPHOLES OPEN FOR MILLIONAIRES AND BILLIONAIRES.
YOU KIDDIN' ME? LOOK AT THIS BUNCH! BUNCHA YAHOOS. OF ALL OF US, IT SHOULD BE YOU IN LAW SCHOOL. TAKE THE TEST.
THIS IS ABOUT AS WRONG AS IT GETS
CONSUMER BANKING - SELLING DEBT TO MIDDLE CLASS FAMILIES - HAS BEEN A GOLD MINE.
I SINCERELY BELIEVE THAT VERY TIME THE U.S. GOVERNMENT MAKES A LOW-COST LOAN TO SOMEONE, IT'S INVESTING IN THEM. THAT'S SOCIAL JUSTICE.

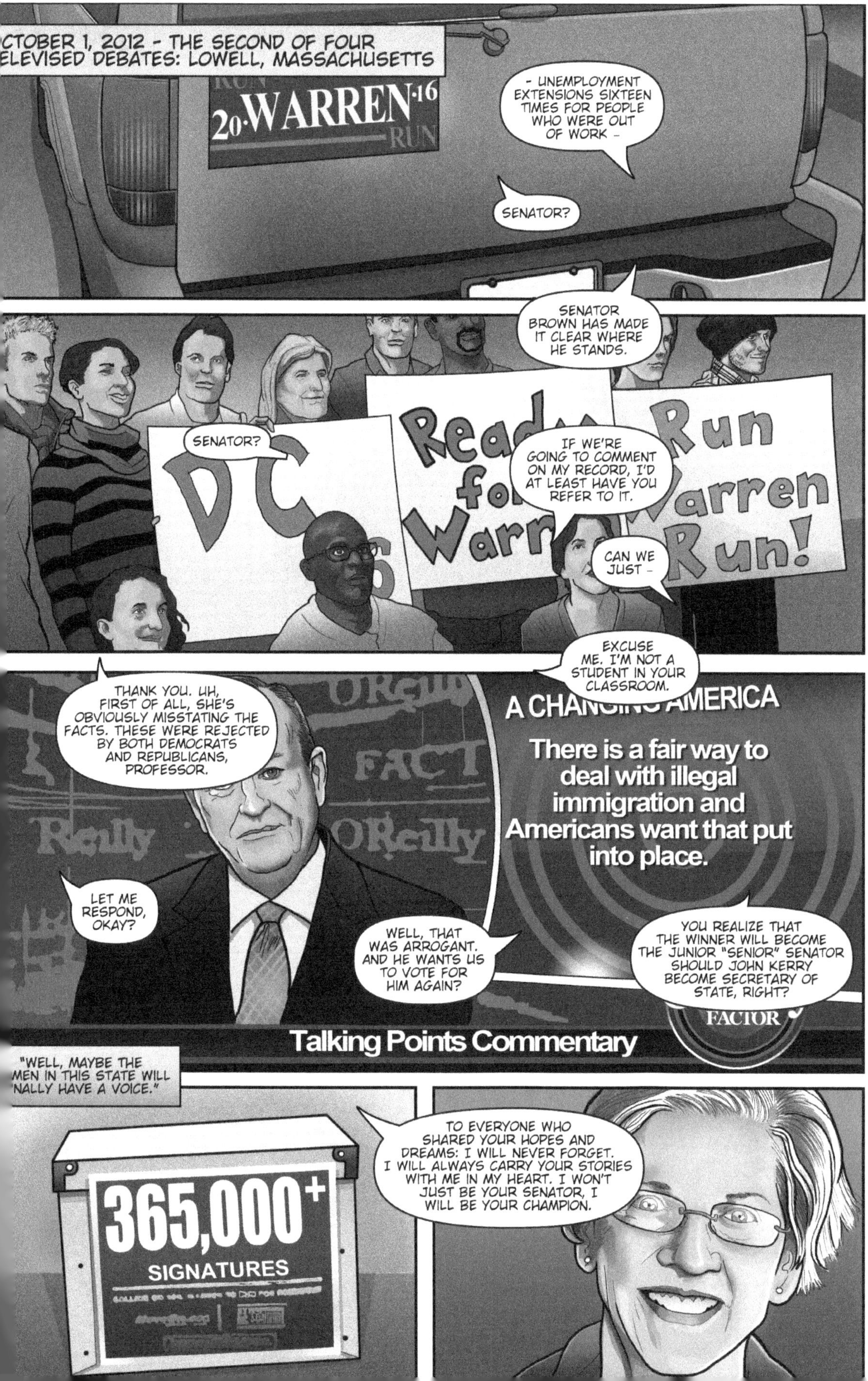
CTOBER 1, 2012 - THE SECOND OF FOUR
ELEVISED DEBATES: LOWELL, MASSACHUSETTS
RUN 20·WARREN·16 RUN
- UNEMPLOYMENT EXTENSIONS SIXTEEN TIMES FOR PEOPLE WHO WERE OUT OF WORK -
SENATOR?
SENATOR?
SENATOR BROWN HAS MADE IT CLEAR WHERE HE STANDS.
IF WE'RE GOING TO COMMENT ON MY RECORD, I'D AT LEAST HAVE YOU REFER TO IT.
Run
arren
Run!
CAN WE JUST -
EXCUSE ME. I'M NOT A STUDENT IN YOUR CLASSROOM.
THANK YOU. UH, FIRST OF ALL, SHE'S OBVIOUSLY MISSTATING THE FACTS. THESE WERE REJECTED BY BOTH DEMOCRATS AND REPUBLICANS, PROFESSOR.
FACT
A CHANGING AMERICA
There is a fair way to deal with illegal immigration and Americans want that put into place.
LET ME RESPOND, OKAY?
WELL, THAT WAS ARROGANT. AND HE WANTS US TO VOTE FOR HIM AGAIN?
YOU REALIZE THAT THE WINNER WILL BECOME THE JUNIOR "SENIOR" SENATOR SHOULD JOHN KERRY BECOME SECRETARY OF STATE, RIGHT?
FACTOR
Talking Points Commentary
"WELL, MAYBE THE
MEN IN THIS STATE WILL
NALLY HAVE A VOICE."
365,000+
SIGNATURES
TO EVERYONE WHO SHARED YOUR HOPES AND DREAMS: I WILL NEVER FORGET. I WILL ALWAYS CARRY YOUR STORIES WITH ME IN MY HEART. I WON'T JUST BE YOUR SENATOR, I WILL BE YOUR CHAMPION.

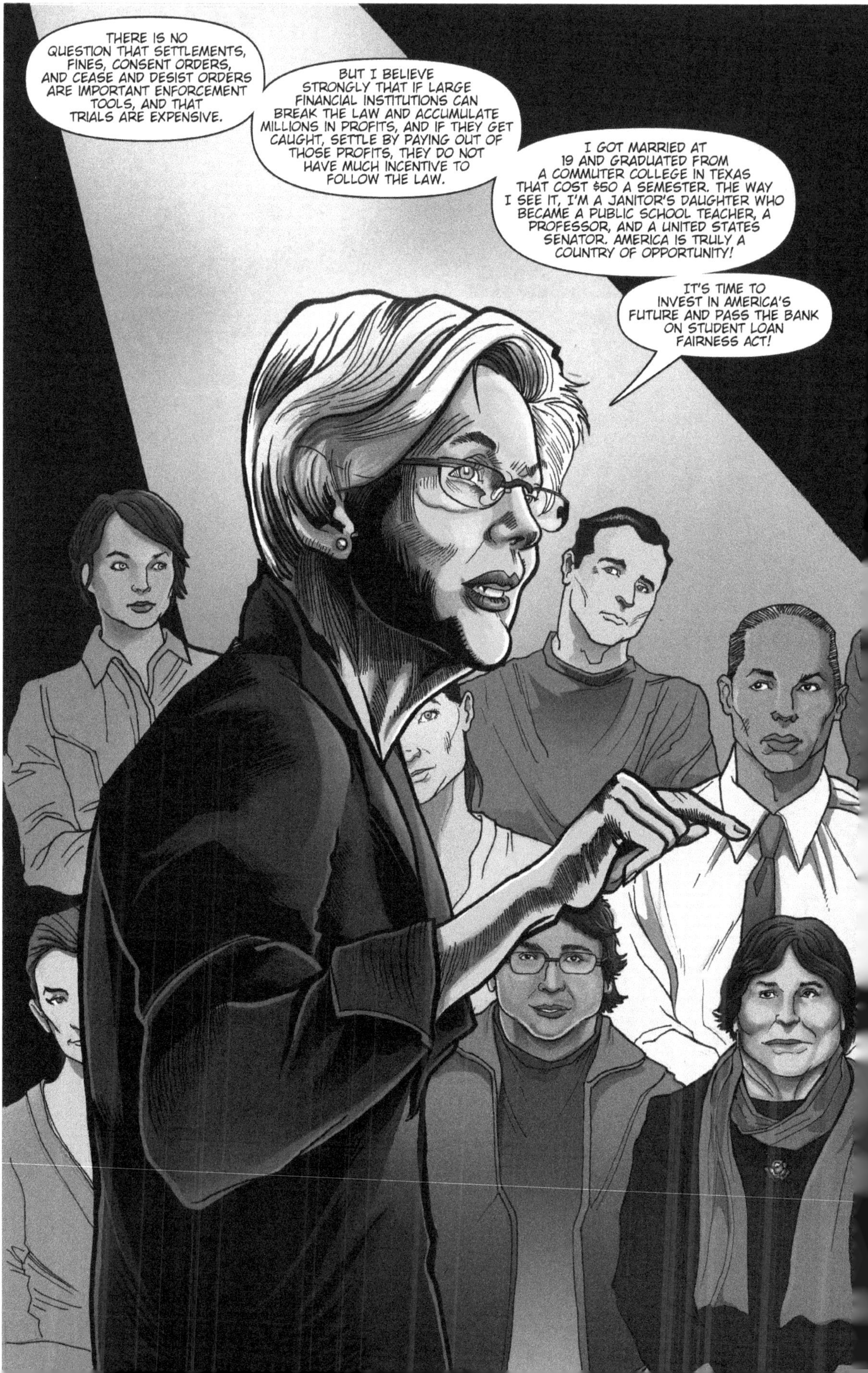
THERE IS NO QUESTION THAT SETTLEMENTS, FINES, CONSENT ORDERS, AND CEASE AND DESIST ORDERS ARE IMPORTANT ENFORCEMENT TOOLS, AND THAT TRIALS ARE EXPENSIVE.
BUT I BELIEVE STRONGLY THAT IF LARGE FINANCIAL INSTITUTIONS CAN BREAK THE LAW AND ACCUMULATE MILLIONS IN PROFITS, AND IF THEY GET CAUGHT, SETTLE BY PAYING OUT OF THOSE PROFITS, THEY DO NOT HAVE MUCH INCENTIVE TO FOLLOW THE LAW.
I GOT MARRIED AT 19 AND GRADUATED FROM A COMMUTER COLLEGE IN TEXAS THAT COST $50 A SEMESTER. THE WAY I SEE IT, I'M A JANITOR'S DAUGHTER WHO BECAME A PUBLIC SCHOOL TEACHER, A PROFESSOR, AND A UNITED STATES SENATOR. AMERICA IS TRULY A COUNTRY OF OPPORTUNITY!
IT'S TIME TO INVEST IN AMERICA'S FUTURE AND PASS THE BANK ON STUDENT LOAN FAIRNESS ACT!

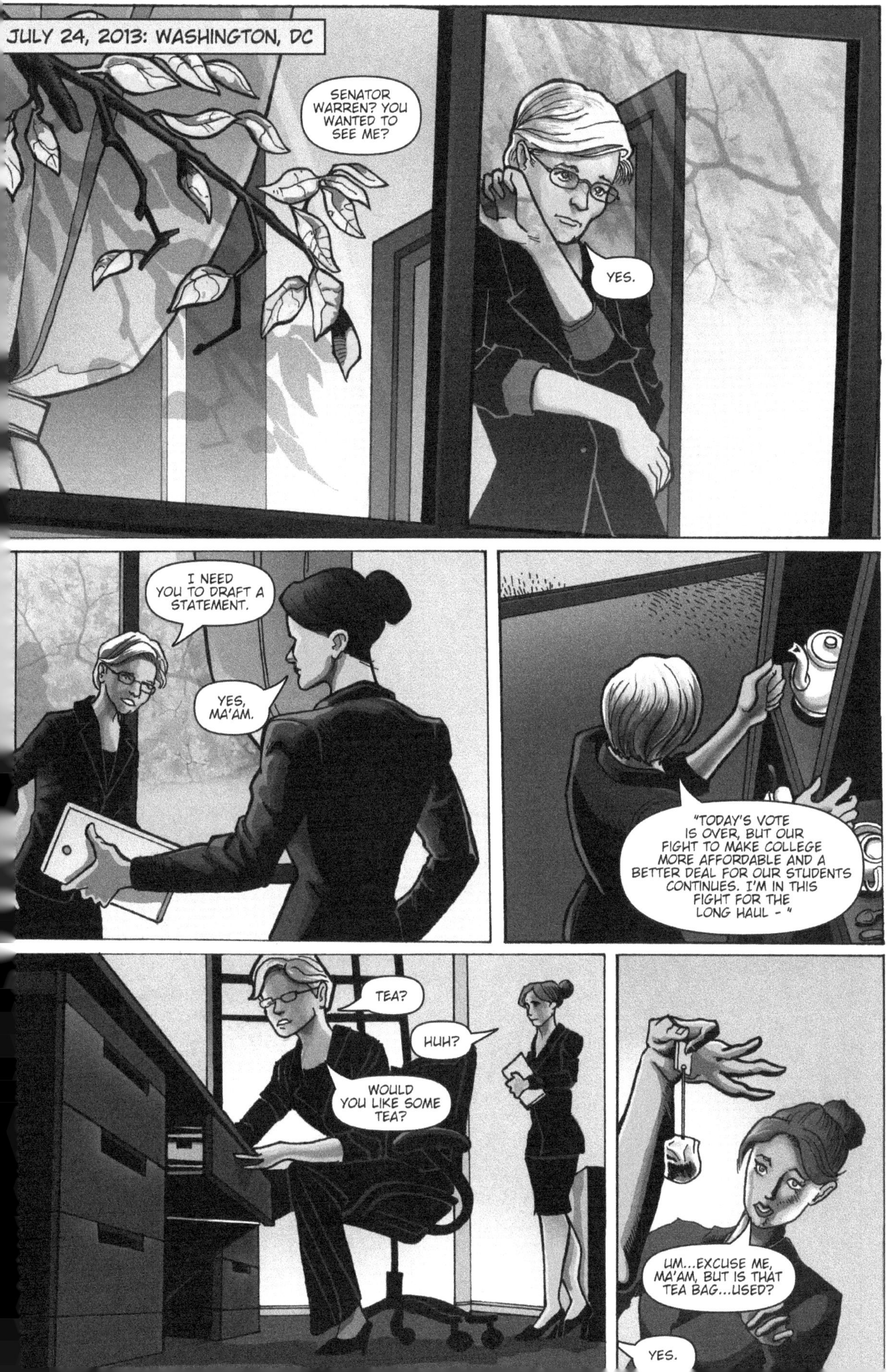
JULY 24, 2013: WASHINGTON, DC
SENATOR WARREN? YOU WANTED TO SEE ME?
YES.
I NEED YOU TO DRAFT A STATEMENT.
YES, MA'AM.
"TODAY'S VOTE IS OVER, BUT OUR FIGHT TO MAKE COLLEGE MORE AFFORDABLE AND A BETTER DEAL FOR OUR STUDENTS CONTINUES. I'M IN THIS FIGHT FOR THE LONG HAUL - "
TEA?
HUH?
WOULD YOU LIKE SOME TEA?
UM...EXCUSE ME, MA'AM, BUT IS THAT TEA BAG...USED?
YES.

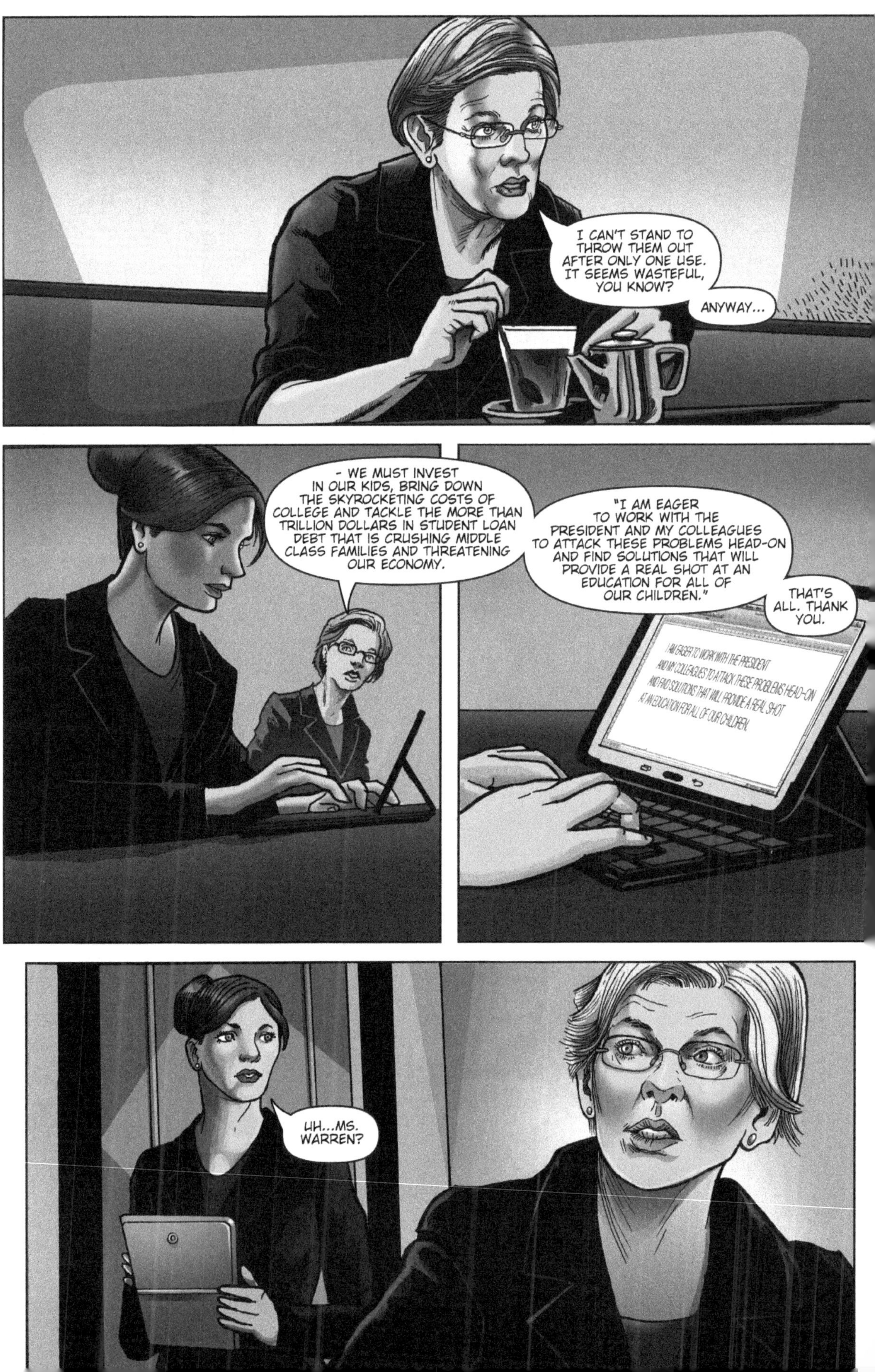
I CAN'T STAND TO THROW THEM OUT AFTER ONLY ONE USE. IT SEEMS WASTEFUL, YOU KNOW?
ANYWAY...
- WE MUST INVEST IN OUR KIDS, BRING DOWN THE SKYROCKETING COSTS OF COLLEGE AND TACKLE THE MORE THAN TRILLION DOLLARS IN STUDENT LOAN DEBT THAT IS CRUSHING MIDDLE CLASS FAMILIES AND THREATENING OUR ECONOMY.
"I AM EAGER TO WORK WITH THE PRESIDENT AND MY COLLEAGUES TO ATTACK THESE PROBLEMS HEAD-ON AND FIND SOLUTIONS THAT WILL PROVIDE A REAL SHOT AT AN EDUCATION FOR ALL OF OUR CHILDREN."
THAT'S ALL. THANK YOU.
I AM EAGER TO WORK WITH THE PRESIDENT AND MY COLLEAGUES TO ATTACK THESE PROBLEMS HEAD-ON AND FIND SOLUTIONS THAT WILL PROVIDE A REAL SHOT AT AN EDUCATION FOR ALL OF OUR CHILDREN.
UH...MS. WARREN?

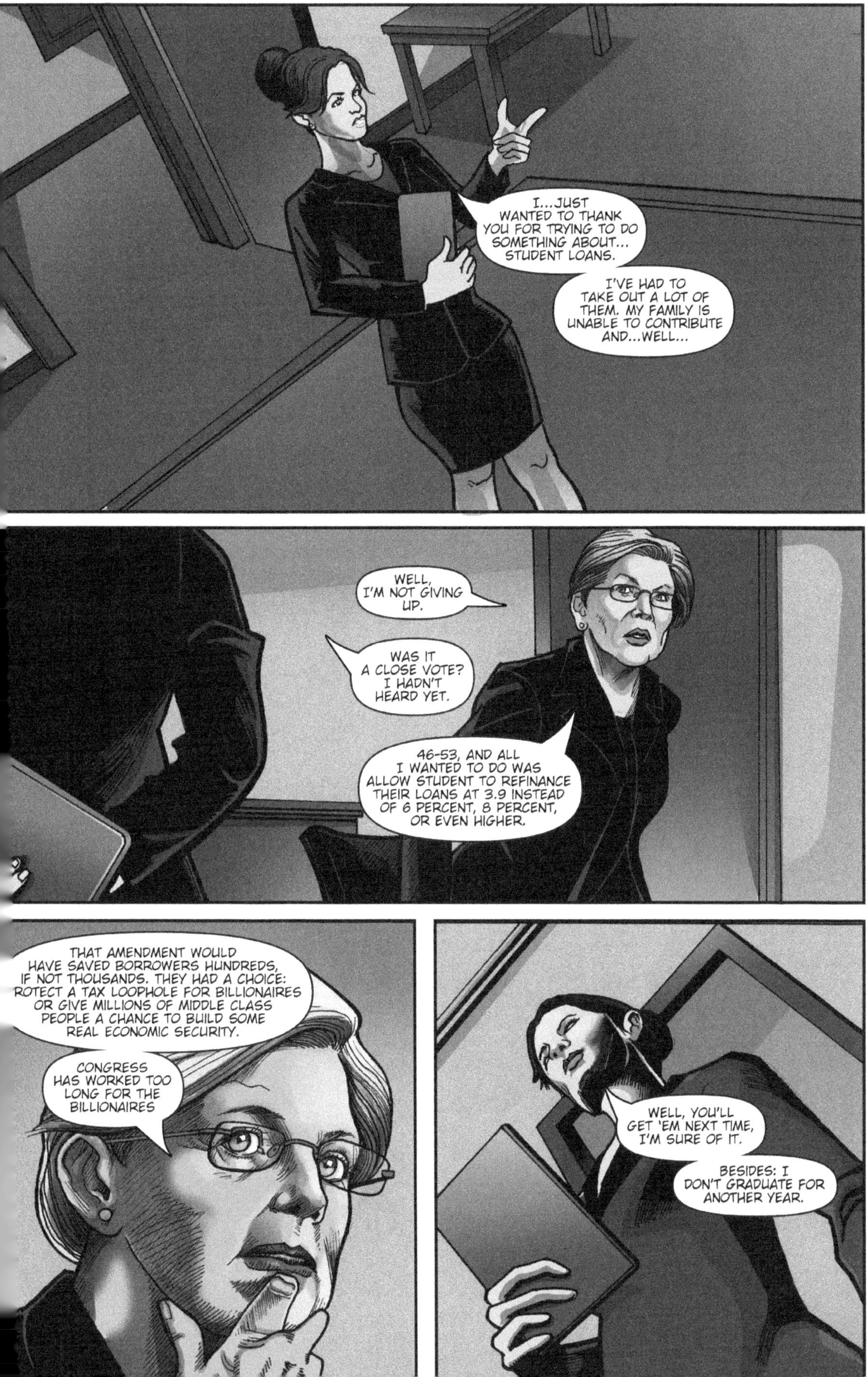
I...JUST WANTED TO THANK YOU FOR TRYING TO DO SOMETHING ABOUT... STUDENT LOANS.
I'VE HAD TO TAKE OUT A LOT OF THEM. MY FAMILY IS UNABLE TO CONTRIBUTE AND...WELL...
WELL, I'M NOT GIVING UP.
WAS IT A CLOSE VOTE? I HADN'T HEARD YET.
46-53, AND ALL I WANTED TO DO WAS ALLOW STUDENT TO REFINANCE THEIR LOANS AT 3.9 INSTEAD OF 6 PERCENT, 8 PERCENT, OR EVEN HIGHER.
THAT AMENDMENT WOULD HAVE SAVED BORROWERS HUNDREDS, IF NOT THOUSANDS. THEY HAD A CHOICE: ROTECT A TAX LOOPHOLE FOR BILLIONAIRES OR GIVE MILLIONS OF MIDDLE CLASS PEOPLE A CHANCE TO BUILD SOME REAL ECONOMIC SECURITY.
CONGRESS HAS WORKED TOO LONG FOR THE BILLIONAIRES
WELL, YOU'LL GET 'EM NEXT TIME, I'M SURE OF IT.
BESIDES: I DON'T GRADUATE FOR ANOTHER YEAR.

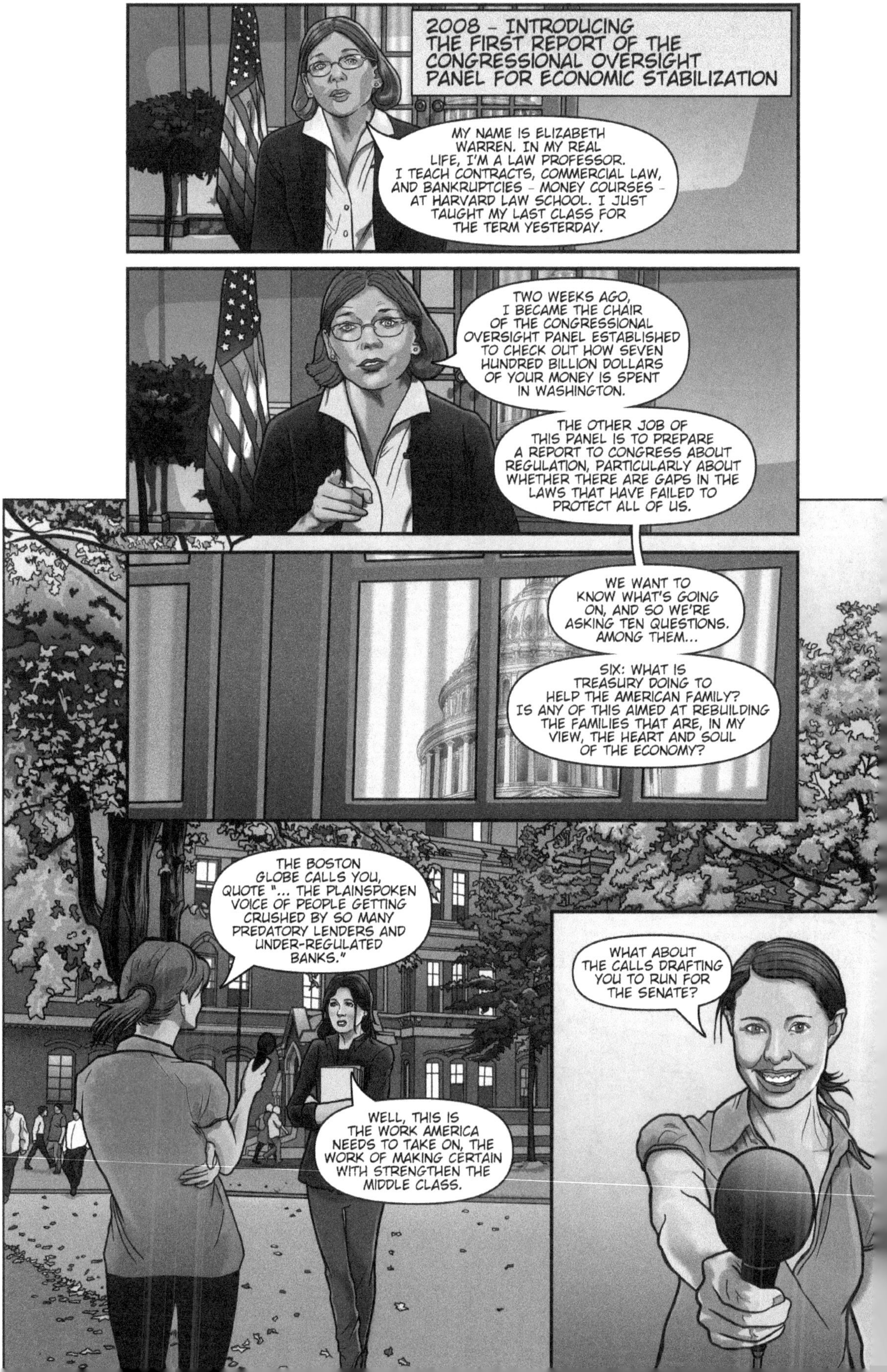
2008 – INTRODUCING THE FIRST REPORT OF THE CONGRESSIONAL OVERSIGHT PANEL FOR ECONOMIC STABILIZATION
MY NAME IS ELIZABETH WARREN. IN MY REAL LIFE, I'M A LAW PROFESSOR. I TEACH CONTRACTS, COMMERCIAL LAW, AND BANKRUPTCIES – MONEY COURSES – AT HARVARD LAW SCHOOL. I JUST TAUGHT MY LAST CLASS FOR THE TERM YESTERDAY.
TWO WEEKS AGO, I BECAME THE CHAIR OF THE CONGRESSIONAL OVERSIGHT PANEL ESTABLISHED TO CHECK OUT HOW SEVEN HUNDRED BILLION DOLLARS OF YOUR MONEY IS SPENT IN WASHINGTON.
THE OTHER JOB OF THIS PANEL IS TO PREPARE A REPORT TO CONGRESS ABOUT REGULATION, PARTICULARLY ABOUT WHETHER THERE ARE GAPS IN THE LAWS THAT HAVE FAILED TO PROTECT ALL OF US.
WE WANT TO KNOW WHAT'S GOING ON, AND SO WE'RE ASKING TEN QUESTIONS. AMONG THEM...
SIX: WHAT IS TREASURY DOING TO HELP THE AMERICAN FAMILY? IS ANY OF THIS AIMED AT REBUILDING THE FAMILIES THAT ARE, IN MY VIEW, THE HEART AND SOUL OF THE ECONOMY?
THE BOSTON GLOBE CALLS YOU, QUOTE "... THE PLAINSPOKEN VOICE OF PEOPLE GETTING CRUSHED BY SO MANY PREDATORY LENDERS AND UNDER-REGULATED BANKS."
WELL, THIS IS THE WORK AMERICA NEEDS TO TAKE ON, THE WORK OF MAKING CERTAIN WITH STRENGTHEN THE MIDDLE CLASS.
WHAT ABOUT THE CALLS DRAFTING YOU TO RUN FOR THE SENATE?

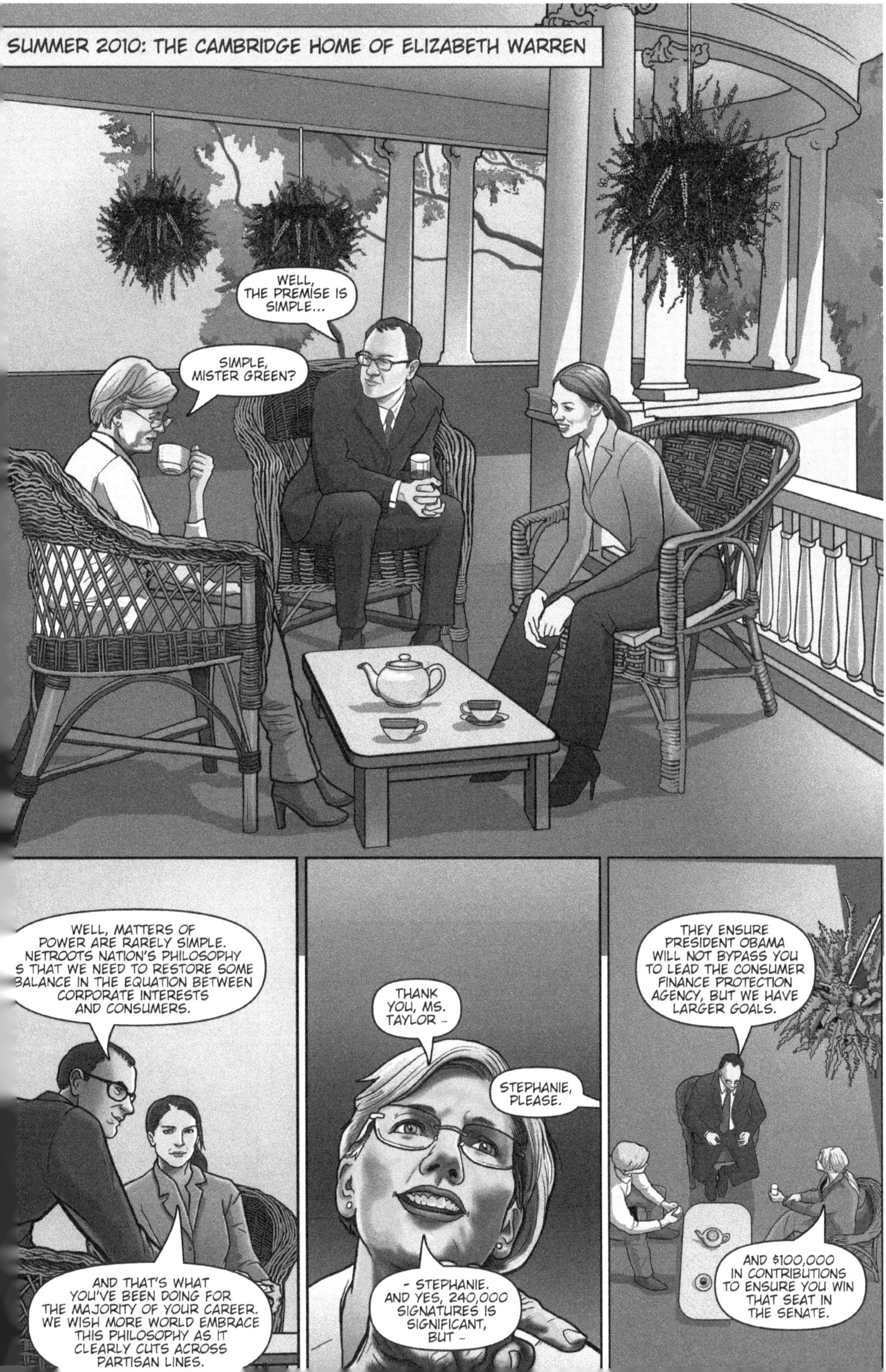
SUMMER 2010: THE CAMBRIDGE HOME OF ELIZABETH WARREN
WELL, THE PREMISE IS SIMPLE...
SIMPLE, MISTER GREEN?
WELL, MATTERS OF POWER ARE RARELY SIMPLE. NETROOTS NATION'S PHILOSOPHY S THAT WE NEED TO RESTORE SOME BALANCE IN THE EQUATION BETWEEN CORPORATE INTERESTS AND CONSUMERS.
AND THAT'S WHAT YOU'VE BEEN DOING FOR THE MAJORITY OF YOUR CAREER. WE WISH MORE WORLD EMBRACE THIS PHILOSOPHY AS IT CLEARLY CUTS ACROSS PARTISAN LINES.
THANK YOU, MS. TAYLOR -
STEPHANIE, PLEASE.
- STEPHANIE. AND YES, 240,000 SIGNATURES IS SIGNIFICANT, BUT -
THEY ENSURE PRESIDENT OBAMA WILL NOT BYPASS YOU TO LEAD THE CONSUMER FINANCE PROTECTION AGENCY, BUT WE HAVE LARGER GOALS.
AND $100,000 IN CONTRIBUTIONS TO ENSURE YOU WIN THAT SEAT IN THE SENATE.

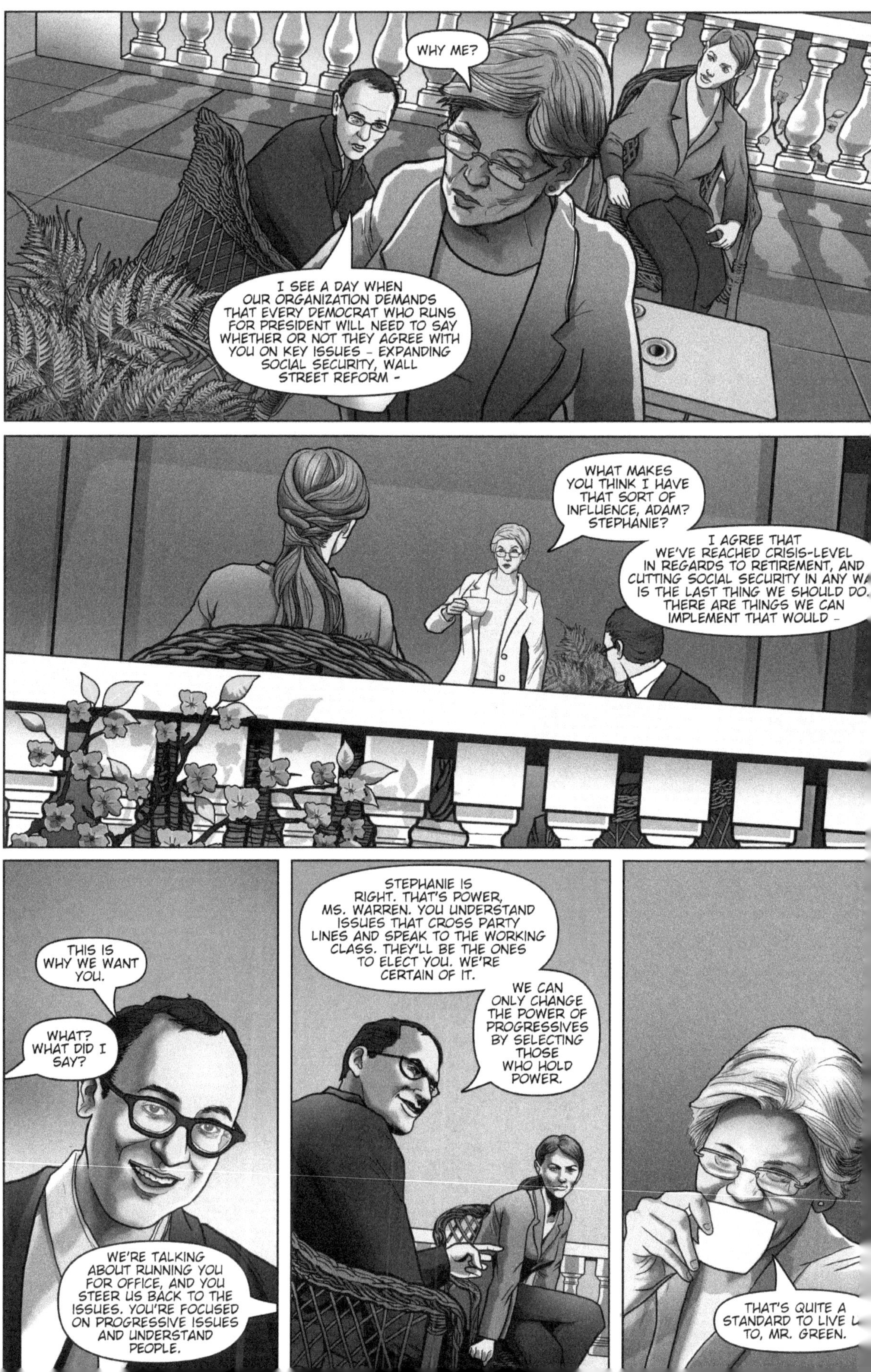
WHY ME?
I SEE A DAY WHEN OUR ORGANIZATION DEMANDS THAT EVERY DEMOCRAT WHO RUNS FOR PRESIDENT WILL NEED TO SAY WHETHER OR NOT THEY AGREE WITH YOU ON KEY ISSUES - EXPANDING SOCIAL SECURITY, WALL STREET REFORM -
WHAT MAKES YOU THINK I HAVE THAT SORT OF INFLUENCE, ADAM? STEPHANIE?
I AGREE THAT WE'VE REACHED CRISIS-LEVEL IN REGARDS TO RETIREMENT, AND CUTTING SOCIAL SECURITY IN ANY WA IS THE LAST THING WE SHOULD DO. THERE ARE THINGS WE CAN IMPLEMENT THAT WOULD -
THIS IS WHY WE WANT YOU.
WHAT? WHAT DID I SAY?
WE'RE TALKING ABOUT RUNNING YOU FOR OFFICE, AND YOU STEER US BACK TO THE ISSUES. YOU'RE FOCUSED ON PROGRESSIVE ISSUES AND UNDERSTAND PEOPLE.
STEPHANIE IS RIGHT. THAT'S POWER, MS. WARREN. YOU UNDERSTAND ISSUES THAT CROSS PARTY LINES AND SPEAK TO THE WORKING CLASS. THEY'LL BE THE ONES TO ELECT YOU. WE'RE CERTAIN OF IT.
WE CAN ONLY CHANGE THE POWER OF PROGRESSIVES BY SELECTING THOSE WHO HOLD POWER.
THAT'S QUITE A STANDARD TO LIVE L TO, MR. GREEN.

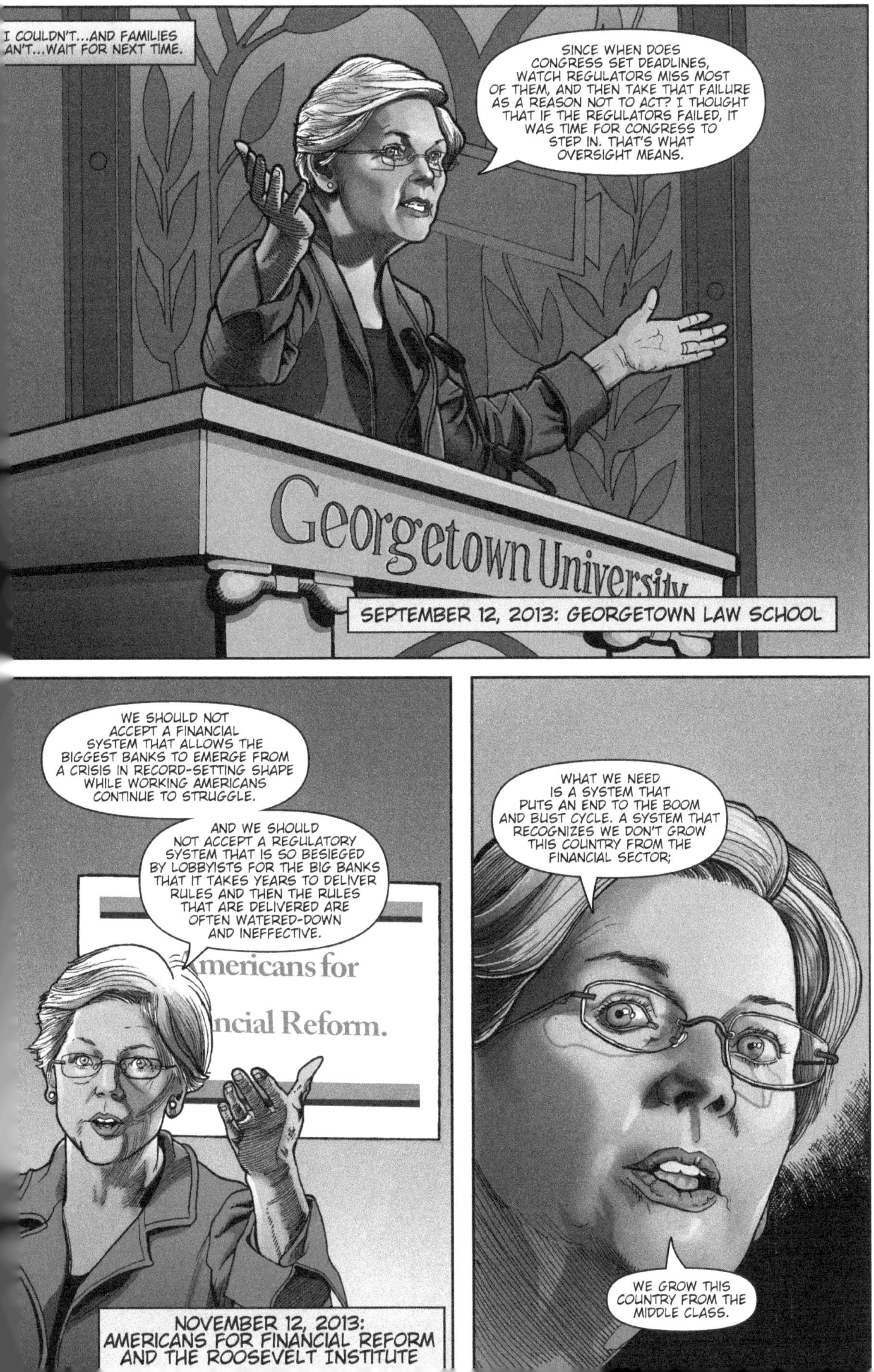
I COULDN'T...AND FAMILIES AN'T...WAIT FOR NEXT TIME.
SINCE WHEN DOES CONGRESS SET DEADLINES, WATCH REGULATORS MISS MOST OF THEM, AND THEN TAKE THAT FAILURE AS A REASON NOT TO ACT? I THOUGHT THAT IF THE REGULATORS FAILED, IT WAS TIME FOR CONGRESS TO STEP IN. THAT'S WHAT OVERSIGHT MEANS.
Georgetown University
SEPTEMBER 12, 2013: GEORGETOWN LAW SCHOOL
WE SHOULD NOT ACCEPT A FINANCIAL SYSTEM THAT ALLOWS THE BIGGEST BANKS TO EMERGE FROM A CRISIS IN RECORD-SETTING SHAPE WHILE WORKING AMERICANS CONTINUE TO STRUGGLE.
AND WE SHOULD NOT ACCEPT A REGULATORY SYSTEM THAT IS SO BESIEGED BY LOBBYISTS FOR THE BIG BANKS THAT IT TAKES YEARS TO DELIVER RULES AND THEN THE RULES THAT ARE DELIVERED ARE OFTEN WATERED-DOWN AND INEFFECTIVE.
mericans for
ncial Reform.
NOVEMBER 12, 2013: AMERICANS FOR FINANCIAL REFORM AND THE ROOSEVELT INSTITUTE
WHAT WE NEED IS A SYSTEM THAT PUTS AN END TO THE BOOM AND BUST CYCLE. A SYSTEM THAT RECOGNIZES WE DON'T GROW THIS COUNTRY FROM THE FINANCIAL SECTOR;
WE GROW THIS COUNTRY FROM THE MIDDLE CLASS.

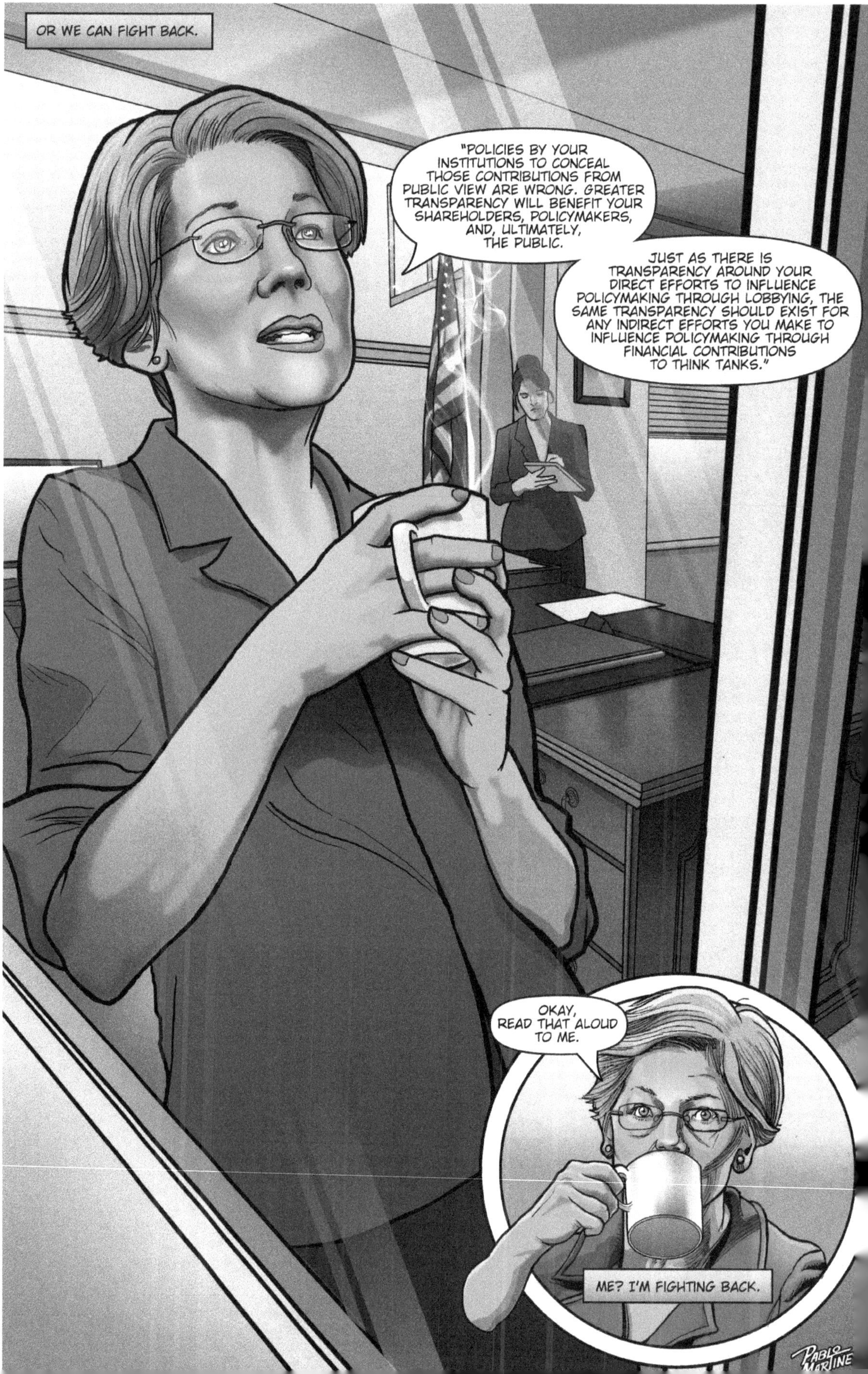
OR WE CAN FIGHT BACK.
"POLICIES BY YOUR INSTITUTIONS TO CONCEAL THOSE CONTRIBUTIONS FROM PUBLIC VIEW ARE WRONG. GREATER TRANSPARENCY WILL BENEFIT YOUR SHAREHOLDERS, POLICYMAKERS, AND, ULTIMATELY, THE PUBLIC.
JUST AS THERE IS TRANSPARENCY AROUND YOUR DIRECT EFFORTS TO INFLUENCE POLICYMAKING THROUGH LOBBYING, THE SAME TRANSPARENCY SHOULD EXIST FOR ANY INDIRECT EFFORTS YOU MAKE TO INFLUENCE POLICYMAKING THROUGH FINANCIAL CONTRIBUTIONS TO THINK TANKS."
OKAY, READ THAT ALOUD TO ME.
ME? I'M FIGHTING BACK.
PABLO MARTINE

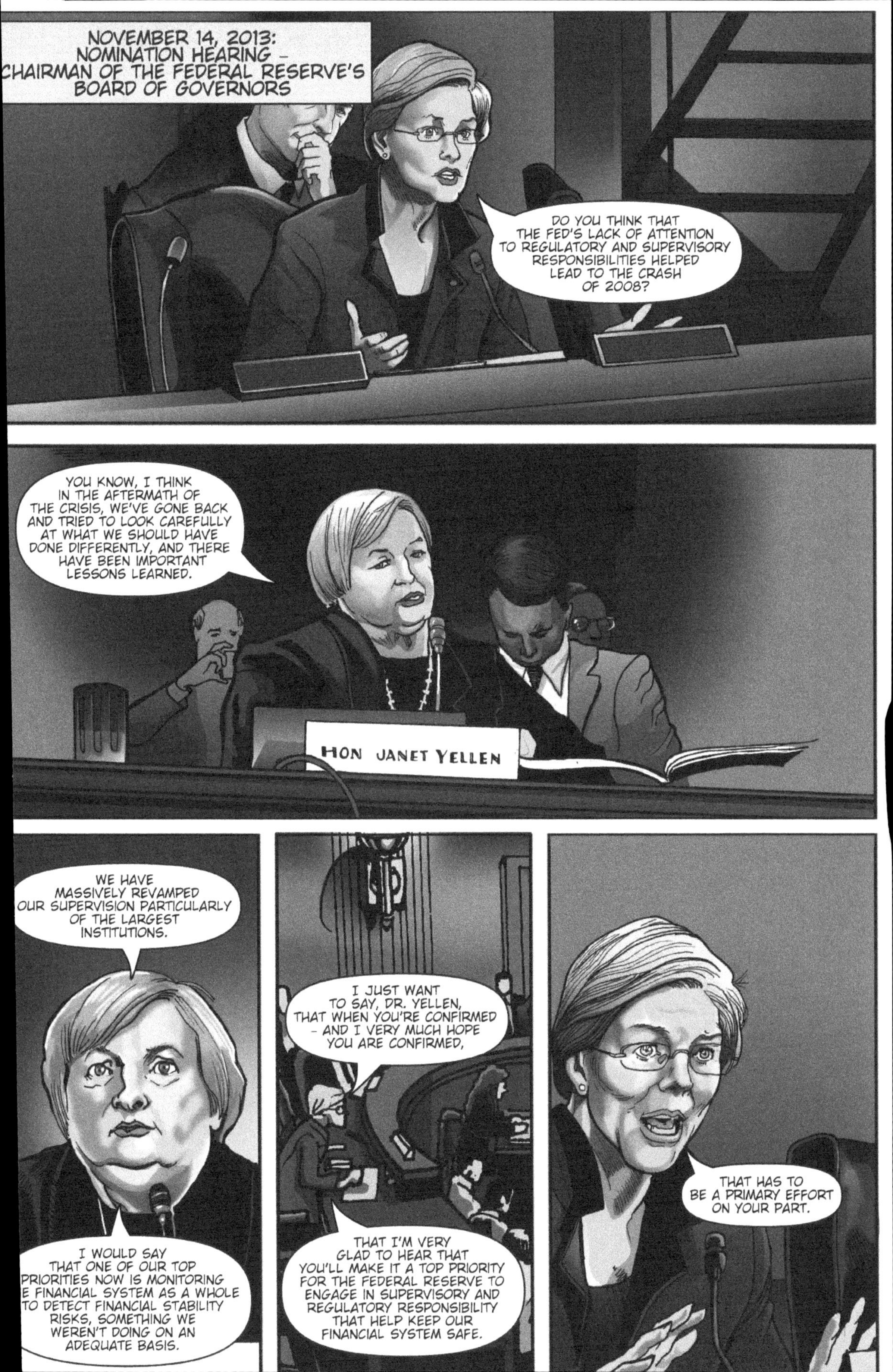
NOVEMBER 14, 2013: NOMINATION HEARING – CHAIRMAN OF THE FEDERAL RESERVE'S BOARD OF GOVERNORS
DO YOU THINK THAT THE FED'S LACK OF ATTENTION TO REGULATORY AND SUPERVISORY RESPONSIBILITIES HELPED LEAD TO THE CRASH OF 2008?
YOU KNOW, I THINK IN THE AFTERMATH OF THE CRISIS, WE'VE GONE BACK AND TRIED TO LOOK CAREFULLY AT WHAT WE SHOULD HAVE DONE DIFFERENTLY, AND THERE HAVE BEEN IMPORTANT LESSONS LEARNED.
HON JANET YELLEN
WE HAVE MASSIVELY REVAMPED OUR SUPERVISION PARTICULARLY OF THE LARGEST INSTITUTIONS.
I WOULD SAY THAT ONE OF OUR TOP PRIORITIES NOW IS MONITORING E FINANCIAL SYSTEM AS A WHOLE TO DETECT FINANCIAL STABILITY RISKS, SOMETHING WE WEREN'T DOING ON AN ADEQUATE BASIS.
I JUST WANT TO SAY, DR. YELLEN, THAT WHEN YOU'RE CONFIRMED – AND I VERY MUCH HOPE YOU ARE CONFIRMED,
THAT I'M VERY GLAD TO HEAR THAT YOU'LL MAKE IT A TOP PRIORITY FOR THE FEDERAL RESERVE TO ENGAGE IN SUPERVISORY AND REGULATORY RESPONSIBILITY THAT HELP KEEP OUR FINANCIAL SYSTEM SAFE.
THAT HAS TO BE A PRIMARY EFFORT ON YOUR PART.

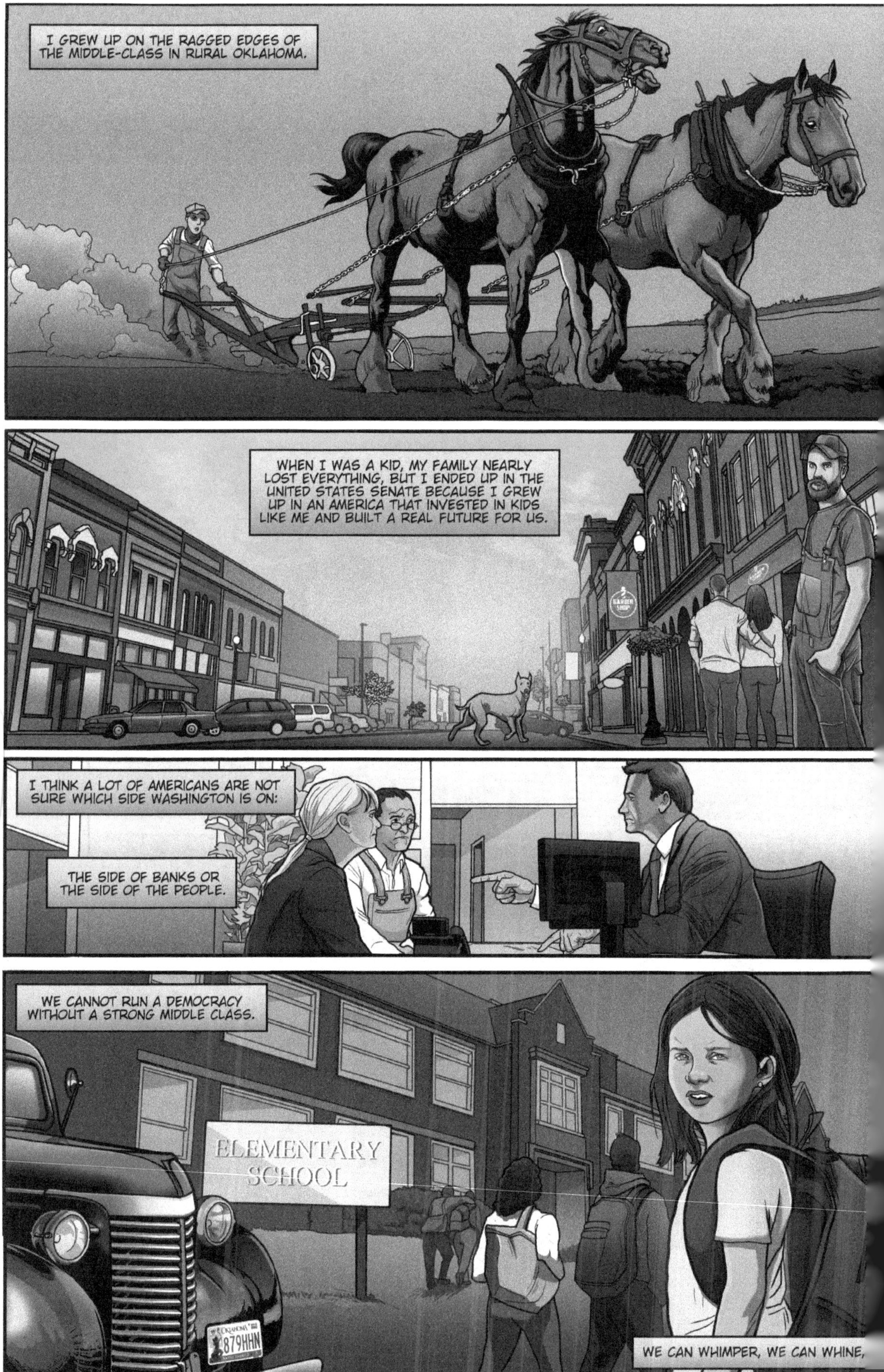
I GREW UP ON THE RAGGED EDGES OF THE MIDDLE-CLASS IN RURAL OKLAHOMA.
WHEN I WAS A KID, MY FAMILY NEARLY LOST EVERYTHING, BUT I ENDED UP IN THE UNITED STATES SENATE BECAUSE I GREW UP IN AN AMERICA THAT INVESTED IN KIDS LIKE ME AND BUILT A REAL FUTURE FOR US.
BARBER SHOP
I THINK A LOT OF AMERICANS ARE NOT SURE WHICH SIDE WASHINGTON IS ON:
THE SIDE OF BANKS OR THE SIDE OF THE PEOPLE.
WE CANNOT RUN A DEMOCRACY WITHOUT A STRONG MIDDLE CLASS.
ELEMENTARY SCHOOL
OKLAHOMA
879HHN
WE CAN WHIMPER, WE CAN WHINE,

TIDALWAVE COMICS

PROGRESSIVE CHANGE
CAMPAIGN COMMITTEE
BOLDPROGRESSIVES.ORG

Michael L. Frizell — Writer

Pablo Martinena & Vincenzo Sansone — Penciler

Darren G. Davis — Editor

Benjamin Glibert — Letterer

Pablo Martinena & Chris Canibano — Colors

**Darren G. Davis**
Publisher

**Maggie Jessup**
Publicity

**Susan Ferris**
tertainment Manager

TIDALWAVE PRODUCTIONS

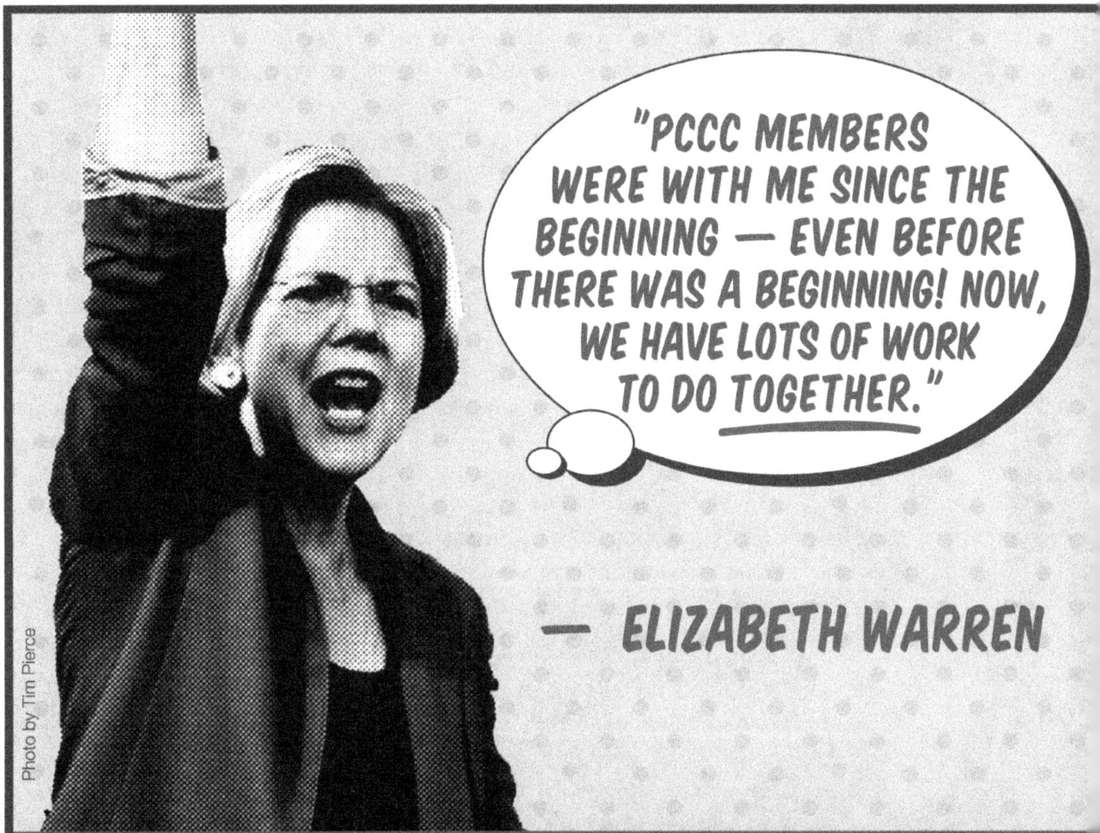
"PCCC MEMBERS WERE WITH ME SINCE THE BEGINNING — EVEN BEFORE THERE WAS A BEGINNING! NOW, WE HAVE LOTS OF WORK TO DO TOGETHER."
— ELIZABETH WARREN
Photo by Tim Pierce